MW00895923

# DELIVERED BY *Grace*

By Beverly Armstrong

ZOË LIFE
PUBLISHING
WORDS TO LIVE BY

Published by:
Zoë Life Publishing
P.O. Box 871066
Canton, MI 48187 USA
www.zoelifepub.com

Author:     Beverly Armstrong
Cover:      Chamira Jones
Editor:     Amber Goddard


First U.S. Edition 2007

Library of Congress Cataloging-in-Publication Data

Armstrong, Beverly.
  Delivered By Grace/ by Beverly Armstrong. -- 1st U.S. ed.
     p. cm.
  Includes bibliographical references.
  ISBN 0-9779445-5-7
  1. Christian life. 2. Salvation. I. Title.
  BV4501.3.A75 2006
  243--dc22
                                    2006016201

13 Digit ISBN 978-0-9779445-5-2

For current information about releases by *Beverly Armstrong* or other releases from Zoë Life Publishing, visit our Web site: http://www.zoelifepub.com

Printed in the United States of America

# v17 06 26 07

# DELIVERED BY *Grace*

By Beverly Armstrong

# Table of Contents

# FOREWORD

*"My son, give attention to my words; Incline your ear to my sayings. Do not let them depart from your eyes; Keep them in the midst of your heart; For they are life to those who find them. And health to all their flesh."* (Proverbs 4:20)

THROUGH THE WRITINGS in this divinely inspired book, *Delivered by Grace,* Beverly Armstrong has emerged on the scene in much the same way that "saviors" of old emerged. First of all, the people rebel against God, and are brought under oppression and grief. Then, they cry out to the Lord in the midst of their confusion and the Lord raises up a deliverer to deliver them. These "deliverers" were a mixture of militant passion, praise, wit, and prophetic articulation.

For such a time as this, God has raised up a prepared deliverer, Beverly Armstrong, who understands the way out of the deep. If you take what she says and treat it like the wise man suggests in Proverbs 4:20-22, both life and health will be your delight.

May God ever bless you, Sister Beverly, for being the gift that you are. You are a Nubian Queen of great and precious value to the hurting masses yet yearning to be free.


Always Yours
In Him,


**Bishop Charles L. Middleton, Sr.**
*Pastor, Mt. Zion New Covenant Baptist Church*
*Detroit, Michigan*
*General Overseer Men's Ministry*
*Full Gospel Baptist Church Fellowship International*

i

# $\mathscr{I}$NTRODUCTION

T HESE "MESSAGES OF deliverance" are divinely revealed from God, through the Holy Spirit, through me, and are designed to allow us to be set free from any bondages so that we may pursue the will and purpose of God. While holding the pen as God led me through the writing and research, much deliverance, revelation, and knowledge have been poured into my life so that I may pour it into yours.

God's will includes God's designed choices, decisions, and lifestyle. God's purpose is the divine assignment that you were carefully designed to fulfill on the earth. His will is your obedience to the Word of God. This obedience shelters you through the storms of life and covers you from constant exposure and defeat from the kingdom of darkness. When you come out from under this covering of obedience, satan can, at that time, guide the direction of your life. To prevent mistaken identity of whose voice you hear, be sure that you are continuously filled with God's Word and filled afresh with God's Spirit.

Your purpose is your God-given assignment, which no one in the world can fulfill except you. In order to recognize what it is, to prepare you for it and pursue the assignment to its maximum potential, you cannot be in bondage. Satan will attempt to infiltrate your life with subtle bondages that are innocent in appearance, but are designed to distract you from bringing this assignment to pass. God designed you for it and it for you. He allows you to go through experiences to prepare and equip you for it. The mixture of your DNA at birth was set for this purpose. If you are not sensitive to the Spirit of God and the Word of God, you will not be positioned for the preparation nor the purpose. It is at that point of your journey that you have permitted satan to take control of your life.

Let's take a look at some of God's biblical characters as examples of satanic interference. Samson's mother advised him not to marry a Philistine. Delilah manipulated him until he told her the secret of his strength. He lost his eyes and his strength to the Philistines. Jonah fled from God's presence to Tarshish when God told him to go to Nineveh to cry out against their wickedness. He did go to Nineveh after being delivered from the fish's belly. Adam and Eve were deceived by the serpent, and from their disobedience came the Fall of Man.

Through God's Word and God's Spirit, *Delivered By Grace* gives you practical tools for you to apply to living, moving, and keeping your being within the realm of obedience. God's Word says that God's people are destroyed for lack of knowledge. Through the direction of the Holy Spirit, God's Word, and my own experiences and research, I have mapped out a plan for your spiritual growth and success in many areas of your life. Be delivered from any distracting bondages and go forward in God's will and purpose for your life. A dying world is waiting…

# 1

# *W*HY DELIVERANCE?
# I AM SAVED!

## WHAT IS DELIVERANCE?

IN ORDER TO prepare your heart and mind for deliverance, you must fully understand what deliverance is and why it is necessary.

> *"And being renewed in the spirit of your mind and that you put on the new man which was created according to God in true righteousness and holiness."* (Ephesians 4:23-24)

The definition of "deliverance" is, "to release from bondage, danger or any kind of evil; to set free from slavery, to put into another's possession of power." Romans 12:2 tells us to be not conformed to this world, but to be transformed by the renewing of our minds so that we can display the good, acceptable, and perfect will of God. Although our transformation is in process, it can be easy for us to fit into the culture and environment around us – the sins that so easily beset us. When we are new believers and have not really "learned of God," we can fall into the pattern of establishing our own righteousness instead of submitting to the righteousness of God.

Adhering to the moral law of the land without a relationship with God and His Word is an act of righteousness that cannot last because it is by might and power. Lasting righteousness must be sealed by the Spirit of God and the Blood of Jesus. As we respond to situations, making decisions and choices, we should be mindful that they line up with God's Word and God's Spirit.

Even if we know the Word of God from Genesis to Revelation, we must learn to apply it as trials, tests, attacks, and difficult situations surface in our lives. If not, we will continue to be conforming to this world. As soldiers in God's army, deliverance represents victory in battle. Yes, the battle is the Lord's, but He wins through His yielded vessels.

God speaks to His people through His Word with confirmation that, even for His saints, His children, and His righteous, we are perfected through deliverance.

*"...keep your tongue from evil and your lips from speaking deceit. Seek peace and pursue it."* (Psalm 34:13)

*"... the righteous cry out and the Lord hears and delivers them out of all of their troubles."* (Psalm 34:17)

*"...many are the afflictions of the righteous, but the Lord delivers him out of them all."* (Psalm 34:19)

*"...take my yoke upon you and learn of Me."* (Matt. 11:29)

*"...My people are destroyed for lack of knowledge"* (Hos. 4:6)

Just these few excerpts of scripture (and there are many others) make it obvious that there is work to do after our born-again experience, our conversion to Christianity. We are still being delivered from our carnal minds, thoughts, and habits. Jesus told His disciples that, if they did not accept His kingdom as a little child, they would not enter the kingdom.

As newborns mature into adults, we must mature from being born in sin and shaped in iniquity to transform to the image of our God.

Non-believers enter truth through accepting Jesus Christ as their Lord and Savior. Their pathway to truth is to confess with their mouth the Lord Jesus and believe in their hearts that God has raised Him from the dead. For, with the heart they believe that Jesus is the righteous one, and with their mouth they confess their sins (Romans 10) and accept conversion through the shed Blood of Jesus.

For born-again believers, truth is manifested both in the Word of God and in our recreated spirit. After our born-again experience, the spirit is saved. Continually, however, the Word of God must cultivate our minds, emotions, thoughts, and feelings.

This continued renewal – deliverance – equips us to handle situations, circumstances, and people-problems in a manner that pleases God. If we believe that we are walking in the Word, but are bound in our spirit, there is a possibility that we have misinterpreted what God is really saying. For example, Ephesians 5:24 says: "Therefore, just as the church is subject to Christ, so let wives be subject to their husbands in everything." That verse does not give the husband license for physical and emotional abuse; the previous verse says for the husband and wife to submit to one another in the fear (reverence) of God. Would God want His creation, His temple of the Holy Ghost, abused?

## WHY DELIVERANCE? THE FALL...

In the beginning, man's condition was one of moral purity, made in the image and likeness of God. There was no evil temperament in man's nature. God gave man an assignment of tending and caring for the garden. Man was blessed with great freedom to receive abundantly from all that God created. God also gave additional directions for their lives – to eat, multiply the earth, and have dominion over all living things. God's only restriction was for man not to eat of the Tree of the Knowledge of Good and Evil. If man had been obedient, he would have retained moral purity, would not have known evil and, thus, would not have become exposed to an environment of sin.

Since the Fall, however, in every dimension of our human experience, we must be delivered from evil. Even after we are born again, we have the sin-inherited right to choose between good and evil. Through the Blood of Jesus, we have overcome the evils of this world. Unfortunately, though, all realms of our existence are vulnerable to environmental influences. Therefore, we must combat the influences of our evil environment by transforming to the purity of God's Kingdom.

## ENVIRONMENTAL INFLUENCES

> *"To understand the truth that a person is a total being is to see that ministry must focus upon every dimension of existence. True ministry is concerned with the spiritual, the social, the physical, and psychological."*
> (Holman)

From the very beginning of our existence, positive or negative environmental influences affect the pathway of our cognitive, behavioral, and cultural development. The fact is that our environment is in existence before we enter our world and continues after we leave. This personal environment dictates ranges of acceptable behavior. How our environment influences us and how we respond to the influences are determining factors in the lives we will lead and the person we become.

As we are exposed to the rules and conduct of our particular family, our interpretation of how life should be is formed. To successfully live in our family environment, we learn to conform to their pre-existing cultural modes of behavior and understanding. We unconsciously accept these customs as we grow into maturity. Thus, our language, beliefs, ideas, customs, skills, and family patterns often remain intergenerational, unless new information is learned and implemented.

- ***Prenatal Influcncc:*** In the past 25 years, researchers have, in many ways, confirmed suspicions that, in the latter months of pregnancy, babies share in the emotions of their mothers. Studies show that babies in the womb have learned to kick in response to vibrations and noises. Connecting the mother's emotional life while pregnant and the personality of the child as he or she matures is a very controversial concept. There are studies, however, which have proven that anxious mothers are likely to birth anxious babies.

  Research suggests that short-term emotional upsets do not have negative emotional consequences. On the other hand, continuous major emotional disturbances throughout the pregnancy can lead to emotionally troubled children. Also, extreme maternal distress has been linked to premature birth and low birth weight.

  Stress produces hormones that effect emotions. It is said that when the fetus gets accustomed to chronic stress, the nervous system makes preparation to overreact to stimuli.

So we see that, even at birth, thought and behavioral deficits can already exist.

- *Infant Environmental Influence:* An infant can actually die from not being shown love and affection. When they are not exposed to an environment in which they feel protected from danger and instability, it is probable that negative thought patterns, negative behavioral patterns, and negative emotional patterns will surface. Their nature is to respond to being loved, protected, and cared for. Consequently, their development is affected in all areas when they are not nurtured.

- *Child Environmental Influence:* Children that are exposed to physical abuse, emotional abuse, violence, and neglect are at risk for having emotional problems. These problems include anxiety, difficulty in establishing relationships, and not feeling good about themselves. These children have a tendency to feel that they are "bad" and worthless. Commonly, helplessness and inferiority accompany these feelings and negative thought patterns develop.

On the other hand, studies show that children in a good environmental climate of being cared for, respected, listened to, and accepted conclude that they are looked upon as "good" and feel good about themselves.

- The *Social Realm* influences our interpretation of family roles, gender roles, professional status, and economic status. We identify our own self worth, public identity, and self-conceptions by comparing ourselves to those that we consider to be in major status positions. Social roles are defined and validated according to cultural standards of influence.

- The *Psychological Realm* of influence has its own domain. It involves development of motivation, perception, intelligence, and emotional responses. These processes include the impact of social forces and the accompanying psychological dynamics of people around them. These dynamics includes influence of emotions, personality traits, cognitive styles, abilities, and behaviors.

- The *Soulish Realm* is of our feelings, wishes, will, and intellect. Prior to the Fall, our spirit was to be the king, the soul was to be the servant, and the body was to be the slave. After the Fall, man's spirit died, his soul became the king, and his body was the servant.

What is the soul? The Dictionary of the English Language's interpretation of the soul is the faculties of thought, action, and emotion, the emotional nature of man as distinguished by his mind or intellect. "Soul" is also described as the entire scale of feelings under the influence of man, even the psychological.

All activities of the Christian involve coordination between our spirit, soul, and our five senses. The *soul realm* activities are controlled by the Holy Spirit. The *soulish* activities are ordered by the Christian's rebellious, environmentally-influenced soul.

Because of the Fall, it is only after our bodies are resurrected and we become spirit bodies that the Spirit will be in total control. Since we are *transforming*, but not totally *transformed*, we have no choice but to interact with the *soulish realm* daily and continuously.

In order to minimize the power of satanic forces, we must add strength to the regenerate spirit through God's Word and Spirit. Also, we must identify our weaknesses in the *soulish realm* as we die daily to the flesh. As the Apostle Paul tells us, "We wrestle not against flesh and blood, but principalities and powers ... spiritual wickedness in heavenly places" (Ephesians 6:12).

- ***The Carnal Mind:*** Deliverance is essential for overcoming carnality of mind. Satan has many of us deceived that the carnal mind is one step down from holy. On the contrary, the carnal mind is enmity against God. Enmity is a deep-seeded hatred in the form of violent acts (sin). Also, enmity represents the strongest implication of active opposition or combat, as between rivals and opponents. Thus, the carnal mind is not and cannot be subject to the law of God.

A carnal-minded person is a slave of the flesh, the world, and the self. He is not recognized as a spiritual man because he is saved from hell through conversion, but not saved from himself. That is why God says to the converted "Take My yoke upon you and learn of Me." In the Hebrew language, the yoke is the totality of the master's attributes.

According to carnal Christian doctrine, holiness is good and commendable, but optional. People who support this doctrine can remain comfortable in the realm of sin.

It is my personal experience that, when you are in Christ, you yearn for more of Him and less of yourself. You desire to be transformed to His righteousness and holiness. Repentance is a necessary component in this process of turning around.

In Christ, sin is no longer our master and we

press toward the mark of the high calling of God in Christ Jesus. Therefore, when we sin, our spirit is disturbed with conviction until holiness is restored. We cannot accept carnality as a mid-ground between righteousness and unrighteousness. Because the Divine Seed of God is at work within us, we will and must pursue this path of wholeness through deliverance.

Well, you may say, "I don't have a carnal mind." Do you seek God's Word and will in every area and situation of your life? According to Romans chapter 8, there are two spheres – flesh and spirit, and two destinies – life and death. Deliverance from carnality will be a continuous process of feeding the Words of Life into our spirits.

> *"While spirit seems to be the dimension whereby humans can cooperate with and respond to God, flesh is that dimension that represents human limitations and weakness."* (Holman)

## ENEMIES OF DELIVERANCE

*"For the weapons of our warfare are not carnal, but mighty in God for pulling down strongholds, casting down arguments and every high thing that exalts itself against the knowledge of God, bringing every thought into captivity to the obedience of Christ and being ready to punish all disobedience when your obedience is fulfilled."* (II Corinthians 10:4-6)

Life's experiences and acculturations to certain emotional climates can lead us into patterns of bondage, and as these patterns of bondage develop, they can birth dysfunctional behaviors and thoughts within us. These conditions are truly Enemies of Deliverance.

Yes, whom the Son sets free is free indeed. Yet, the flesh wars against the spirit and the spirit against the flesh. Therefore, we must put on the whole armor of God in order to stand against these enemies of freedom or wiles of the devil.

Just as God has blessed the physical health professionals with healing processes, He has also blessed the mental health professionals with healing processes also. These cognitive and behavioral tools give us the knowledge to identify and combat these enemies of deliverance.

To prepare your hearts and minds to be "Delivered By Grace," we will focus on four enemies – strongholds, guilt, passive behaviors, and distorted thought patterns.

- **Strongholds** are walls constructed to defend ungodly actions such as wrong behaviors, wrong ways of thinking, and wrong beliefs. These strongholds are erected to shield sinful ways from the truth of God and to justify disobedience to God. Whatever you use to justify your ungodly action is a stronghold. They serve as walls between you and your relationship with God.

    Strongholds are strengthened through consistent disobedience to God without repenting and turning. Many of us ignore God's command from Ephesians 4:26: "*… do not let the sun go down upon your wrath.*" As we continually deny our disobedience by rationalizing and justifying it rather than accepting the truth of God's Word, we put a strong shield between truth and ourselves. In order to make the lie true over time, the stronghold gets stronger. As people around us identify strongholds and as they try to penetrate the bondage by speaking truth, they are looked upon as attackers.

More strongholds are erected to defend the ones already in existence. Even when we recognize the stronghold for what it is, we have defended it so much that we are ashamed to back down. Through deliverance, the enemy's logic, justification, and reasoning must bow down as our lives transform to the will, knowledge, and Spirit of God.

Instead of continuing to erect strongholds to protect our lies, Christians have the power to tear them down. How? By drawing nigh to God, casting our cares upon Him – resist satan and he will flee. When we draw nigh to the truth of God, satan is powerless in our lives. As we draw nigh to God, He will strip us of rebellion in the form of pride, bitterness, and stubbornness. Yes, it is rebellion against God when we refuse to obey Him because we insist that we are right about something that does not line up with His Word. As God imparts truth into our unyielded situations, we must surrender our minds, wills, and emotions to Him. Because strongholds are lies, the wall can be penetrated only through repentance. Be delivered.

- *Passive Behavior* is also an enemy of deliverance. Are you a person who withholds your opinions, ideas, or thoughts for fear of upsetting others? Do you often feel like a human doormat?  Do you try to please others to the extent that you say "yes" when you mean "no?" Do you have problems expressing your feelings openly and honestly?  Do you often feel helpless and hopeless?

     If the answer to any of these questions is yes, you are probably vulnerable to or in the bondage of passive behavior.  This style of behavior is developed through fear of not being accepted and lack of self-worth and self-confidence. Through the course of life, the passive person has compromised their rights as a person to accommodate others.  Some of these rights are as follows:

- the right to be heard

- the right to be respected

- the right to pursue your own goals and dreams

- the right to your own values, beliefs, opinions, and emotions

- the right to tell others how you wish to be treated

- the right to say "No," "I don't know," "I don't understand," or "I don't care"

- the right to change your mind

- the right to make mistakes

- the right to like yourself even though you're not perfect

- the right to do less than you are capable of doing

- the right to enhance your life

In order to be free to fulfill your purpose in God, you must consider your own opinions, judgments, and needs to be as important as those of others. You are wonderfully, gloriously, and uniquely made by God. You must consider the person you are when you respond to the events and circumstances of your life.

Remember that you have the right to your opinions, decisions and a right to say no without excuses. Instead of searching for different responses when the other person is being persistent, just repeat their last response and repeat your response.

> Example: *I understand all that you have said, but I feel disrespected when you treat me that way.*

Knowing who we are, walking in Christ, and walking in our rights as an individual starts us on the road to combating passive behavior. Additionally, we must clearly express our thoughts and feelings by speaking the truth in love.

Understand why passive behavior is such an enemy to deliverance. People-pleasing puts your priorities out of God's divine order and will. You are to first please God, not others. When pleasing God and yourself is against what others require of you, you feel guilty and confused. You don't think you deserve to be pleased. Thus, it is uncomfortable to you. It is my experience that when you do what is pleasing to God, you will be pleased. Then everything and everyone else will fall into place.

> *"For do I now persuade men, or God? Or do I seek to please men? For if I still pleased men, I would not be a bondservant of Christ."* (Galatians 1:10)

- **Guilt** is another enemy of deliverance. As Christians, it is healthy for us to feel conviction, remorse, and regret for our wrongdoing. These are indicators that we are godly sorry enough to refrain from repeating the wrong. They are accompanied by energy to do better, because the focus is on the behavior and not the person. Guilt, on the other hand, implies that we are what we did. Thus, it is followed by feelings of worthlessness, inferiority, and fear. To condemn ourselves for a wrong is an implication that we are expected to be perfect, all-knowing, and all-powerful. Ask forgiveness from God and the victim of the offense. Then assess the wrong to keep it from happening again. After that, move forth in victory.

> *"There is therefore now no condemnation to those who are in Christ Jesus, who do not walk according to the flesh, but according to the Spirit."* (Romans 8:1)

- ***Distorted Thought Patterns*** are, in my opinion, the most destructive enemies of deliverance.  These thought patterns are in partnership with all emotional attacks on our freedom.

    God's Word says that we should think on whatsoever things are just, pure, lovely, and of good report (Philippians 4:8).  The Word of God is pure and true.  However, because of our deep-rooted, foundational, illogical thought patterns, we have difficulty applying God's truth to our illogical misconceptions.

    > *"God has not given us the spirit of fear and timidity, but of power and of love and of sound mind."*  (II Timothy 1:7)

    In III John 1:2, God tells us that His desire is for us to prosper and be in health, even as our thought life prospers. Illogical, distorted thoughts are birthed from these unconfirmed, irrational beliefs, which are self-induced lies that we form within our own minds. We make assumptions without rationale, input or logic.  Then we use these assumptions as judge and jury to formulate illogical thoughts, ideas, perceptions and conclusions.

Examples:

- If someone finds fault with me, they are never in error.

- My accomplishments determine my value as a person.

- If I do not excel at all times, I am worthless.

- It is essential for me to be faultless so that I can gain others' approval; and, if I can't, I will, in some way, be punished.

- The disapproval of others proves that I am a failure.

The following is a scenario of illogical reasoning, unconfirmed beliefs, and reasonable responses. It is my prayer that this concept of combating illogical thought patterns will bless your life as it did mine.

- ***Illogical Reasoning:*** Mr. C. turned down my summer program recommendation. Certainly, he thinks that

I have no regard for the agency's budget and that I am not capable of being a Master's Level Professional and a responsible person.

- **_Reasonable Thought:_** Although he turned down my recommendation, it does not mean that he thinks less of me as a professional. After all, he is responsible for managing his budget wisely. I cannot assume that his confidence in me has changed, especially without asking him. Besides, imperfections in a project do not determine my value.

- **_Illogical Reasoning:_** However, because of his position in the agency, if he does consider me unprofessional and inconsiderate, it has to be true.

- **_Reasonable Thought:_** It is his prerogative to modify the proposed schedule, and he did approve 80% of it. Yet, to categorize me as unprofessional because I designed it would be an unfair misconception. After all, I was successful in finding a good, free summer program and I am making good progress with my clients. Therefore, I do have some good professional abilities. Besides, I am making all of these assumptions without even asking him what he thinks of me as a professional. He expressed that the program is good except for one adjustment.

- ***Illogical Reasoning:*** If he really does consider me unprofessional and inconsiderate, he will expose me to others and I will no longer be able to function as a professional and as a person.

- ***Reasonable Thought:*** I was functioning as a professional and as a person before entering the Human Services field. Who I am professionally does not determine who I am inwardly. I will not be punished just because I am not faultless.

- ***Illogical Reasoning:*** Actually, I often miss the mark in every area of my life. So I do not really deserve to be accepted professionally or personally.

- ***Reasonable Thought:*** No one is perfect and I am no exception. Not excelling at all times does not make me worthless. I will not give up on myself and I will enjoy my life and enjoy being me while I pursue excellence in all areas of my life. When I miss the mark, tomorrow is another day and, as long as there is life, there is hope. Even above that, I can do all things through

Christ who strengthens me (Philippians 4:13) and I am accepted in the Beloved according to the Word of God (Ephesians 1:6).

Replacing "should" statements with "can" statements for us and others can produce a healthier thought life.

Examples of should statements are:

- What I do and say should be flawless.

- I should always be able to rectify or modify my circumstances immediately.

- I should always be correctly in line with the standards of others.

- I should always present myself in a way that will influence and affect others.

- People should always see things and do things my way.

- People should always acknowledge my efforts.

- Life should be free of favoritism and partiality.

- Life should be without difficult situations.

Replace "should always" in your statements to "can usually" or "can sometimes." In doing this, you will position yourself for a more peaceful life. If not, you are at risk of becoming extremely upset when you or others do not meet your "should" expectations.

To avoid this kind of distress, decide:

- Situations are regrettable, not disastrous

- To accept personal deficiencies; do not always place the responsibility on others

- To handle the load that life dumps on you

There is no rational reason for people or situations to always meet up to your values.

If you recognize that you frequently utilize illogical reasonings in your life, replace them with reasonable thoughts supported by the Word of God.

*"For as he thinks in his heart, so is he."*
(Proverbs 23:7)

By guarding your heart from illogical thoughts, you will be able to avoid guilt, doubt, demonic influence, worry, anxiety, and fear.

Arise! The focal point of deliverance is that we be free for God to fulfill His purpose through our lives. Bound soldiers cannot fight!

> *"And the Lord will deliver me from every evil attack and preserve me for His heavenly kingdom. To Him be glory forever and ever."* (II Timothy 4:18)

> *"... being confident of this very thing, that He who has begun a good work in you will complete it until the day of Jesus Christ."* (Philippians 1:6)

# 2

# $\mathscr{G}$RACE FOR A GODLY FOUNDATION

*"NEVERTHELESS, GOD'S SOLID foundation stands firm, sealed with this inscription: 'The Lord knows those who are His,' and 'Everyone who confesses the name of the Lord must run away from wickedness.'*

*In a large house there are riches, not only of clay; some are for noble purposes and some for ignoble. If a man cleanses himself from the latter, he will be an instrument for noble purposes, made holy, useful to the Master and prepared to do any good work."*
(II Timothy 2:19-21 NIV Study Bible)

"Though it is possible to be saved, yet in need of deliverance, without the foundational salvation of the heart, there can be no real and permanent deliverance."

*-Beverly Armstrong, Author*

If you have not accepted Jesus Christ as your Lord and Savior, that is your first step of deliverance. In order to denounce the reign of the kingdom of darkness in your life, you must be saved. To be saved, you must confess with your mouth the Lord Jesus and believe in your heart that Jesus was born of a virgin, lived a sinless life, was faultlessly crucified, rose from the dead, and is seated at the right hand of the Father. At this point, we become positionally sanctified as God's building; we are God's temples because we are in relationship with the Father. As we pursue the process of yielding to the Holy Spirit in our lives, we partake in progressive sanctification as we are conformed to the image of Christ.

"Grace For a Godly Foundation" addresses the foundational attributes of God's Kingdom, such as holiness, the Blood of Jesus, and surrendering to God's will and purpose. Prior to our elevation to the next level, we must allow God to form within us these foundational anchors. Can you imagine a high-rise building with a shaky foundation? It would fall and shatter everything in it and around it. Just as a natural building must have certain foundational elements, likewise must we.

# THE IMAGE OF GOD IN YOU

*"In Him we have an inheritance, being predestined according to the purpose of Him who works all things according to the counsel of His will, that we who first trusted in Christ should be to the praise of His glory."*
(Ephesians 1:11-12)

Man was made in God's image. This means that we are reproductions of His very appearance, a reflection of His very character. God made us to be the embodiment of His perfect example to the world. In order for us to represent Him, He endowed us with all of His attributes.

When sin entered the world, man did not lose God's attributes. Man did, however, become vulnerable to the kingdom of darkness. At that point, man became exposed to choice. Making the right choice after sin entered was complicated, because yielding to the flesh added an ungodly sphere to God's creation. The body (flesh) was made only to display His image within us. After man yielded to the flesh through disobedience, resulting from disbelief in God's Word, flesh gained access to our hearts. This access interrupted and divided man's pleasure in God's perfect righteousness. Instead of absolute solitary pleasure in the nature of God, pleasure was also found in the ungodly sphere of the flesh.

It is difficult for me to relate to people within the Body of Christ who say they are bored and not excited about their lives. Truthfully, I cannot even imagine someone being a bored or restless Christian. There is just too much work to be done. If you fall into this bored, restless category, however, that is a good indication that you are not walking in God's purpose for your life. Just preparing for your God-given assignment of reaching out to the lost takes considerable time from each day. Studying God's Word and praying is a full-time commitment and a necessary one as you allow God to equip you for the ministry that He has assigned to you.

God has singled each of us out to fulfill His purpose. He created us in His mind for a specific time and place on the earth before we were conceived in the womb. As He permits us to experience certain challenges, He is molding us into who we have become and are becoming.

More good news is that God's image and His attributes are still within us in spite of the Fall of Man. Prior to salvation, they are covered up by sin. Once we believe and change our minds through repentance, our trust is no longer divided. Jesus' nature alone is in our hearts because His shed blood is daily crucifying the flesh.

Actually, we are becoming who we already are. Studying our purpose in the article "Christian Tree of Life," I learned something fascinating. Leaves do not change to their beautiful reds, oranges, and yellow colors in autumn. They already have those colors. However, during the spring and summer, the true color is covered by green chlorophyll cells that come off during the autumn season. The leaf's true color is then unveiled.

Our sanctification parallels this concept. We were born in sin and shaped by iniquity. When we accepted Jesus as our Savior and Lord, His attributes were restored within us. After we grow in the Lord, learn of Him, and shed the old nature through deliverance, His glory that is already in us is displayed to the world. Our godly nature, the true color of our hearts, is unveiled.

Through us, God will shine His marvelous light for the lost to see. He has given us unique ways to reach the world that no one else possesses. You will display His glory and give Him a place to lay His head through "The Image of God In You."

## The Image of God in You

God made us in HIS image
And in HIS likeness too
Let us explore now –
Why HIS righteous desire
For His image and likeness in you

"Man will have dominion," God said
"Over every creeping thing
He will be an expression of my heart and my mind
He will display My glory
He will sing"

"With the likeness of My nature
He will bring Heaven into the earth
I, myself, will plant Him a garden
While he names things for me and gives birth"

"I know he will fall
But I will make a sacrifice
Of My one-of-a-kind Son
For man's eternal life"

"Then he will trust Me to be his Savior
As My Spirit draws him, he will make haste
He will turn from the world, accept My love
And My amazing grace"

"Jesus, My Son, will be Lord in the earth
As man seeks My face in prayer
He will destroy spiritual wickedness in heavenly places
As his prayers war against the evils of the air"

"I will always have sweet communion with man
For he can relate to me
He will sup with Me
I will sup with him
He will honor My sovereignty"

"He will destroy principalities and powers
Tear down strongholds in spiritual warfare
He will understand My Word enough to know
His Kingdom assignments of love and prayer"

"For prayer brings My Kingdom in Heaven
And in Earth on one accord
Prayer combats the kingdom of darkness
Its power manifests My position as Lord"

"Man will carry out My plan for him
That My Spirit will reveal
For he bears such a strong resemblance to Me
My purpose he will seek to fulfill"

God says, "Die to self
Come alive to Me
That is what you must do
Give Me a place to lay my head
On the image of Me (God) In You!"

# TEST OF FAITH

> *"But without faith it is impossible to please Him, for he who comes to God must believe that He is, and that He is a rewarder of those who diligently seek Him."* (Hebrews 11:6)

Through a combination of Webster's dictionary and God's Word, faith is defined as a belief in what God says without proof from natural senses (seeing, hearing, touching, feeling). By faith, we accept what God says as truth in spite of the circumstances. Faith requires our certainty in receiving God's Word through our spiritual eyes. Because God's thoughts and ways are higher than ours, the result of our faith doesn't always meet the world's standards of success. God will always, however, prove that He is trustworthy and true to His Word. Your faith will increase as you hear and study His Word. Abraham, the Father of Faith, experienced seasons of doubt when the world was in its fallen state. Since then, Jesus overcame the world through the shedding of His blood; therefore, we are really without excuse.

Faith is believing God's Word, believing that He has

the power to perform it, and is watching over it to perform it. As my former Pastor, Bishop Charles Middleton Sr. says, "Act like God told you the truth." Faith is not only to know the truth intellectually, but to submit to truth's guidance and control. Jesus says, "If you ask anything in My name, I will do it" (John 14:14). As Christians, we should respond to difficult situations using our prayer mode, not our crisis mode. Our belief should not be in what everyone else says, but in what God says.

Many of us in the Body of Christ do not neglect to assemble for worship services. We are faithful stewards to bible study, bible conferences, and prayer meetings. As we, the people of the Most High God, delight ourselves in Him, He will give us the desires of our hearts. It is not necessary for us to accept negative situations and conditions when we can exercise our faith through prayer and ask God to change our situations. Let us not be guilty of having a form of godliness and denying God's power. God did not intend for us to be fat in the Word so that when the storms come, we allow the fat to drip from our spirits to the outer courts of our hearts.

We say that the winds and the waves obey God's will. Yet we accept the weather report as if it is Bible without asking God for the sunshine we want. Earlier this year, rain and thunderstorms were in the weather forecast the day of my dear sister in Christ's poolside bridal shower. In faith, I asked my Heavenly Father to hold back the storms and the rain. During the shower, God blessed us with sunshine and blue skies. There was not a drop of rain until well after the bridal shower ended. God says we have not because we ask not, and when we do ask, we often do not believe that God hears us and that He will move on our behalf.

Through hearing the Word of God, we have faith, but we must protect it. The enemy of our soul, satan, is an opportunist. He will assign doubters and pessimists to us in an attempt to drain our faith. As stated in an old hymn of the church, "I dare not trust the sweetest frame, but wholly lean on Jesus' name." We must recognize attacks on our faith in spite of the sweet, loving vessels through which they come. Our family members, friends, and/or loved ones are usually not maliciously seeking to discount our belief in God's faithfulness to us. They are merely assessing the situation at their level of faith. Unless, we look at situations with our spiritual eyes instead of the natural eye, it is easy to be influenced by what they say and what we see. These natural perspectives are what the Bible refers to as, "... sins which so easily beset us." It is essential that we protect our faith by recognizing when it is under the enemy's attack and that we confront the attack by feeding God's Word into our spirits. The enemy's plot can only be successful if we allow doubt and unbelief to influence our thoughts and belief in what God's Word and the Holy Spirit are saying to us. Truly, we cannot always protect our ears from doubt, disbelief, and negative concepts. However, we do not have to let them influence our faith by allowing them to infiltrate our hearts and our spirits. Our faith acts as a shield to protect negative thoughts from being conceived and nurtured within us.

God has allowed me to identify plots and assignments of the enemy against my marriage, household, relationships, and family. As I go into spiritual warfare by pleading the Blood of Jesus over the situations and praying without ceasing, God fights the battle and the enemy is defeated.

God has given us anointed pastors who are after His own heart. He gives them Words of life to minister to us. Let us not listen to these messages week after week without manifestation of spiritual maturity in our faith. Honor God and the man or woman of God by believing what God is saying through them. Let the Word change how you approach obstacles and tests. As we walk it out, we will be victorious. Will YOU pass the "Test of Faith?"

> *"Well said. Because of unbelief they were broken off, and you stand by faith. Do not be haughty, but fear."* (Romans 11:20)

*"I have been crucified with Christ; it is no longer I who live, but Christ lives in me; and the life which I now live in the flesh I live by faith in the Son of God, who loved me and gave Himself for me."* (Galatians 2:20)

*"For as the body without the spirit is dead, so faith without works is dead also."* (James 2:26)

## *Test of Faith*

Oh, Christian, Oh Christian
Have you not heard?
In order to please our Most High God
Must believe His Word

God has given us all a measure of Faith
Must believe what He said
Without corresponding action (WORKS)
Your faith is dead

Unbelievers may faint in crisis
You cannot respond the same
Christ Himself placed His Word so High
Even above His Name

Your response may be
"I believe His Word"
Have read the Bible through and through
So you have gone through the Bible
But has the Bible gone through you?

Seen it happen, even with myself
Crisis comes
Word goes back on the shelf
By hearing it, it is hidden in our hearts
So believe it, act on it
Do not fall apart

It's alive and waiting to respond for you
Ready, willing to see you through
In every situation, great or small
The Word is living within you to respond to your call

Activated by faith the Holy Spirit
to give you rest
Faint, fall apart?
No – pass the test

Through the flood, through the storm
God watches over His Word to perform
You will see that the battle is not yours
Through the eyes of faith it belongs to the Lord.

# HOLINESS

> "*I speak in human terms because of the weakness of your flesh. For just as you presented your members as slaves of uncleanness, and of lawlessness leading to more lawlessness, so now present your members as slaves of righteousness for holiness.*" (Romans 6:19)

There is nothing mystical or complicated about holiness. It is merely displaying the character of God through the knowledge of the Word of God by the power and the direction of the Spirit of God. Maintaining fellowship with God is the foundation of maintaining His holiness or His character. Communication with God through prayer is an uncompromisingly necessary factor for fellowship with God. During our prayer time, and as unrighteousness interrupts this fellowship, we must repent and have a repenting spirit. With a spirit of repentance, we are godly sorry for our disobedience to God. Our belief is that by God's power, we can turn and walk in total deliverance from the sinful deed. Studying and meditating on God's Word daily gives us fresh insight as to what does and does not please Him. Daily we must be filled afresh with God's Spirit and clothed with His armor.

Holiness is not confined to a place, person, situation or circumstance. It is the lifestyle for the Christian that Jesus literally died for. Only through the shed Blood of Jesus can we maintain holiness through repentance. For all have sinned and come short of the glory of God (Romans 3:23).

Holiness is put on the back burner when we establish our own righteousness and ignore the righteousness of God. Only God is all-knowing, all-powerful, and omnipresent. When we make our own rules, we can decide that they are useless and that we can get rid of them. We must not establish our own righteousness, but submit to the righteousness of God. Instead of focusing on how we look to other people, we must assess how our actions measure up to God's Word. Man looks at the outward appearance, but God looks at the heart. (I Samuel 16:7). God hates a proud and haughty spirit.

As Christians, we are too often listeners of God's Word, and even students of the Word, but we are not doers of the Word because we fail to apply it to our situations. Thus, we cover our wrongdoing with lies so we do not have to face the truth about ourselves.

Deceiving ourselves into thinking that there is a mid-ground between holy and unholy is a lie of the enemy. No man can serve two masters; for either he will hate one and love the other, or else he will be loyal to the one and despise the other. (Matthew 6:24). If we are not displaying God's character, we are displaying the character of satan. Even a seemingly good deed is disobedience if it is done without God's direction.

A teachable spirit will be our key to deliverance. Pray for patience and kindness in your love walk daily or you will be vulnerable to fleshly actions. Give some thought to how our holy God really hates sin. Godly, sorrowful, true repentance cannot occur if we are more concerned about how what we have done appears to man, rather than how it appears to God. Jesus shed His blood for sin and overcame the world. Therefore, we do not have to bow down to the bondage of sin. He is waiting for us to repent and turn uncompromisingly to His "Holiness."

> *"For if the firstfruit is holy, the lump is also holy; and if the root is holy, so are the branches. And if some of the branches were broken off, and you, being a wild olive tree, were grafted in among them and with them became a partaker of the root and fatness of the olive tree, do not boast against the branches. But if you do boast, remember that you do not support the root, but the root supports you."* (Romans 11:16-18)

## *Holiness*

Pursuing holiness we're too often defeated
Is displaying God's character such a chore?
For we, the blood bought, the Spirit-filled
Who really love the Lord?

We're faithful to God's purpose
To prayer and God's Word
Yet, the enemy lurks boldly around us
And far too often gets us stirred

Then we feel defeated
Missed the mark again
But is our concern how others look upon us?
Or how our Holy God hates sin?

With a self-centered agenda
True holiness will not make sense
Holiness is being a slave to God's Word
Through lives of obedience

When we sin, God's law is broken
His authority is despised

His government is rated worthless
Is ungodliness worth this price?

Sins are neither large nor small
God hates them however and whenever
Standards of obedience are not measured by the act
But by the majesty of the lawgiver

Oh, Lord, the sovereign majesty of the universe
How majestic is Thy name in all the earth!

# A New Me

> *"Behold, I will do a new thing, now it shall spring forth; Shall you not know it? I will even make a road in the wilderness, and rivers in the desert."* (Isaiah 43:19)

$A$ny time something new exists, there had to have been something old. Therefore, it is most appropriate that before you become acquainted with "a new me," you will understand her a lot better by becoming familiar with "the old me." Attributes that the old and new "me" have in common are being saved, sanctified, and Holy Ghost-filled. Yet, the "old me" was in bondage and the "new me" is free from bondage.

Your question may be, "How can you be saved and be in bondage?" When you are born again, your spirit is saved. But if you do not renew your mind by allowing God to tear down strongholds and destroy yokes, the enemy will monopolize your mind. Probably my greatest stronghold was my addiction to the approval of man. If my decisions and actions did not please others, my emotions would be crushed.

First of all, I wanted everyone to recognize the fact that I was a new creature and speak well of me. Secondly, my desire was to be unapproachable, because I doubted my ability to respond to confrontation in a godly way. Therefore, I considered people-pleasing my security blanket to avoid confrontation and maintain the consistency of peace.

But, glory to the Lamb, the fear of God is the beginning of wisdom (Psalms 111:10). Without righteousness and truth, there can be no real peace. What is peace? My answer would be that it is submitting to the righteousness of God. The Bible says, blessed are the peacemakers for they shall be called the sons of God. This indicates that peacemaking is a process. If there are conflicts or differences, communication must take place. If not, silent disagreement will exist and fester. Conflict can be constructive if properly addressed. Prayerfully assess the issue at hand. Seek a biblical-based, creative solution to the problem. Consider the viewpoint and circumstances of the other person as well as yourself. Calmly speak the truth in love.

Because peacemaking is a mediation process, effective peacemakers must:

- Be encouragers of others, and build others up.

- Be associated with joy. According to Proverbs 17:22, a cheerful heart is good medicine, but a crushed spirit dries up the bones.

- Be filled with the Holy Spirit, because it is through the Spirit that our character is made peaceful.

- Have courage, because we cannot depend on security and safety.

- Have the ability to observe and investigate effectively, so that the appropriate approach is given the matter at hand.

- Persevere by following through on the reconciliation process with humility, knowing your role as servant of God.

- Be willing to confront others, even if it results in a temporary interruption in harmony and relationship.

- Have discernment to assess motives as well as facts.

- Accept people as they are, but encourage them to please God through their attitudes and behaviors.

Truth suppressed, righteousness oppressed is a pathway to depression and oppression, and leaves you vulnerable to severe enemy attacks. God's solution is not people-pleasing, not avoiding confrontation, but speaking the truth in love. My God-given ability to speak the truth in love, to be honest and not artificial, is what brought about "A New Me."

## *A New Me*

I am sorry
She is gone
She will not return
She who previously tried to be everything
for everybody all the time
Now only tries to be something
for some people some of the time
She, who reconstructed her daily plans
for every whim and wish of others
Now, under normal circumstances,
sticks to her plan

She, who could not say no
without feeling guilty
Now, says no in love without guilt
And with the confidence
that when you are in divine order
Following your God-given instincts
Everything and everybody falls into place
She, who exercised false humility
by saying what she thought others
wanted to hear rather than what she really felt
Now expresses true feelings in their beauty and purity

She, who before had to be validated
by her own stipulated external conditions
Is now a whole person

When the house is out of order, and when wrong,
Wrong, disorder and shame no longer go hand in hand
Repentance replaces shame

If I reach my goal, fine
If I miss the mark right now,
I am still God's workmanship
Wondrously and gloriously made

I can say no for the reason
that I just don't choose to do that
No other
And you will still love me tomorrow
If you ever loved me

You can try to manipulate me
But I am aware of what you are doing
Sometimes I will allow you to, other times I won't
I will never again allow you to dominate my life,
my time and my thoughts

So this is the new version

The recharged, revitalized, in control,

genuine version of me

If you preferred the old version

I am sorry

She is gone

She will not return

For my Lord has designed "A New Me"

## BEYOND CONTROL

> *"For do I now persuade men, or God? Or do I seek to please men? For if I still pleased men, I would not be a bondservant of Christ."* (Galatians 1:10)

A good example of a woman being on a mission to carry out God's plan is the Shunamite woman (II Kings 4). First of all, she dispelled the myth that God does not give His vision to His women, for God gave her the vision to feed Elisha and prepare him a room. She, in turn, shared and coordinated the vision with her husband in submission to his covenant headship. She approached her husband, either without fear of criticism or in spite of fear of criticism; and they were able to bless Elisha, the man of God, who in return prophetically declared her heart's desire of a son. When the son became ill, the father immediately sent him to his mother, thus yielding the situation to her authority. When the husband questioned later why she was going to the man of God when it was not the new moon or the Sabbath, she merely said, "It is well." She did not stop to explain that the child was dead or stop to express her plan. This woman was driven by God

60

to do whatever necessary for the hand of God to be upon her family through the man of God. She did not stop to get further sanction or opinion as she humbly went forth in her God-ordained assignment with diligence, and diligently, she remained in God's will. When Elisha instructed the servant, Gehazi, to go to the child and lay Elisha's staff on the dead child's face, the Shunamite woman told Elisha, "As the Lord lives and your soul lives, I will not leave you." In other words, she said, "You must go to my dead son and I will not leave without you." Gehazi's obedient attempts did nothing for the child, but after Elisha's attempts, the child sneezed seven times and opened his eyes.

When our ways please God, we are pleased and, if others are not pleased, God will help them to understand. God created us to glorify Him and fulfill His purpose in our lives. People sometimes have their own agenda for our lives. Seek God for your direction, and when man's agenda clashes with God's agenda, you must be "Beyond Control."

## *Beyond Control*

You will not control me
It is not your job
For I am a follower
Of the Most High God

I must honor you
But must follow HIS lead
When your will is not His will
To His voice I must heed

As much as I love you
Cannot yield to strife
You gave me love
He gave me life

When you have a need
I will try to fulfill,
But my first priority
Is God's divine will

For it is through His will
That I am set free

Through His Spirit
I have liberty

Know we have wisdom
Know we are strong
But in our humanness
We can look at things wrong

When I seek God's face
He puts things in place
And I go as He leads me to go
If what you want
Is not what He wants
Remember – I am
BEYOND CONTROL

# SPIRITUAL ANEMIA

> *"In Him we have redemption through His blood, the forgiveness of sins, according to the riches of His grace."* (Ephesians 1:7)

Blood has such an important function in the human body. It is literally liquid tissue and touches every single cell in us. Actually, it is the only bodily fluid that is not contained in certain areas of the body. Blood is a servant of the body.

White blood cells are like militia, continuously defending the body against outside invaders. They are always on the lookout for signs of disease. When a germ or infection enters the body, the white cells race toward the scene of the crime, which is why swelling occurs. These cells swallow up and kill the germ or infection. As they accomplish their mission, they die in the process and are expelled from the body, along with the infection, in a material that we call pus.

Red blood cells carry oxygen-rich hemoglobin and nutrients from the lungs to all areas of the body. Well, we know what happens without oxygen. We die! So, let us consider the people of the world – the spiritual body. Can you imagine red blood cells contaminated by sin touching every cell of the body? What if the white cells were contaminated by sin and unable to identify and protect the body against the invasion of the kingdom of darkness? Instead of absorbing the sin and leaving the body, what if the sin continued to fester within our hearts with no way of escape?

But there is a way of escape. As the songwriter says, "There is a fountain filled with blood drawn from Immanuel's veins and sinners plunged beneath that flood lose all of their guilty stains." This blood gives us strength from day to day. It never loses its power. It is finished!

What does "It is finished" really mean? It means that God became human through the virgin birth because only a human being can be punished for the sins of a human. Christ lived a sinless life so that He could impart righteousness unto us, allowing us to be charged with His perfect righteousness. That is the only way that we can fellowship with the Holy God. Because sin demands death, Jesus had to be a human because God cannot die. Yet, He had to still be God, because only God can forgive sins, thus delivering us from the powers of sin and death. He had to gratify His own justice and sanctify the offering. That is why Jesus' mother could not have sexual relations with a man prior to His birth. He had to be conceived by God, the Holy Spirit. Jesus had to be a human who could pour out His blood, die, and rise again, so that we can have resurrection life – so that we can live again.

Life is in the blood. Therefore, the shedding of blood exemplifies pouring out life. Christ died a bloody death as an outward evidence that He was sacrificed, a visible display of God fulfilling His promise to save us from sin. As He washed our sins with His pure blood, He transformed our hearts from evil to purify the hearts of all who believe. God's wrath was poured on Jesus that we might have an everlasting covenant of reconciliation. Our fellowship with God is eternally restored. It is finished! Jesus shed His pure blood, died, and arose with all power so that our minds, bodies, and spirits could be washed in the pure, sinless, uncontaminated blood of the Lamb. Because of that blood, we will never have to experience "Spiritual Anemia."

## *Spiritual Anemia*

Mama was sick
Must learn about anemia in a hurry
Needed the knowledge to share with her
So she would not have to worry

Blood hemoglobin low
Weak in mind, body, spirit
Had to learn about blood
So she would not fear it

Anemia not a disease itself
A disorder causing insufficient production
Or condition causing loss of blood
Or excessive red blood cell destruction

Noticed that after the blood transfusion
More strength, appetite returned
Less mental confusion

Lots of praying
Believing the Lord
That the blood come under authority
Of God's Word
Doctor said take iron

Eat and eat
Disorder has had to bow down in defeat

Spiritual blood cells must also be replaced
As the cells are produced in the marrow of faith
Mind tissues renewed with the oxygen of the Word
Spiritual transfusion as the Word is heard

Through the minerals of the Spirit
Through the vitamins of prayer
Cells of faith replenished
Spiritual fatigue no longer there

No need for spiritual anemia
Blood Jesus shed was pure
For those who are washed in this precious Blood
Its power is the cure

To shed this blood, God gave His Son
For Spiritual Anemia – The battle is won
Life's cares can drain us
To the need for replenish

Draw from the fountain
It is filled – IT IS FINISHED.

# 3

# $\mathscr{G}$RACE FOR A GODLY WALK

"*THIS IS THE message which we have heard from Him and declare to you, that God is light and in Him is no darkness at all. If we say that we have fellowship with Him, and walk in darkness, we lie and do not practice the truth. But if we walk in the light as He is in the light, we have fellowship with one another, and the blood of Jesus Christ His Son cleanses us from all sin.*" (I John 1:5-7)

"As long as one allows their walk in the light to be penetrated by every whim, request, and desire of those who walk in darkness, one will never arise to God's desired level and will live in the shadow of the darkness which binds their sanctioned intruders."

*-Beverly Armstrong, Author*

The person walking in darkness does not necessarily have to be an unsaved person. Their dark place can be their lack of knowledge as to who you are in God, where He is taking you, and the time and space necessary in order for you to flow in your assignment.

As you protect your time, space, and energy, you abort the plan of the enemy. To do that, you must make adjustments to anyone who is crowding it. God has another solution to their situation. Be filled with the Spirit and He will teach you and guide you. God will show you how to show love without enabling your loved ones. Seek God's face and He will teach you to empower them instead. Rest assured by faith that, just as the eagle stirs his nest so that his young will learn to fly, our relatives and friends will learn to stand alone once we curtail our enabling behavior.

Some of us are in bondage because of our misinterpretation of the real meaning of love and hate. The NIV Study Bible translation confirms my passion in this area by defining love and hate as attitudes expressed in actions. Can an act of obedience to the needs of others be considered an act of love when it is in disobedience to God's Word? As Christians, we are often distracted by what we consider "acts of love" when in reality, we are entertaining wickedness of the kingdom of darkness and restricting the flow of the purpose of God in our lives.

As we allow our light to shine before men, we must not allow it to grow dim by crowding our lives, our homes, and our space with the agenda of those roaming in utter darkness. Psalms 1:1 refers to us walking not in the counsel of the ungodly, not sitting in the seat of the scornful. Our delight must be in pleasing God with the faith that He will make our peace with man.

## WHERE BONDAGE ENDS

*"Not everyone who says to Me, 'Lord, Lord,' shall enter the kingdom of heaven, but he who does the will of My Father in heaven. Many will say to Me in that day, 'Lord, Lord, have we not prophesied in Your name, cast out demons in your name, and done many wonders in Your name?' And I will declare to them, 'I never knew you; depart from Me, you who practice lawlessness!' "* (Matthew 7:21-23 NKJV)

*"For this is the love of God, that we keep His commandments. And His commandments are not burdensome. For whatever is born of God overcomes the world. And this is the victory that has overcome the world – our faith. Who is he who overcomes the world, but he who believes that Jesus is the Son of God?"* (1 John 5:3-5)

God mightily uses the body of Christ as His vessel to call people out of darkness into His marvelous light. Proclamation of God's Word and personal study of the Word brings the born-again believer into growth, maturity, and increased faith. Revelation from God's Word strips us of the old nature, habits, attitudes, and bondages that were attached to us prior to salvation. If we are, indeed, taking His yoke upon us and learning of Him, we are indeed followers of Christ. There is, however, in my humble opinion and divine revelation, an unsurrendered area that many of us, as believers, have in common. It is the area of total surrender to God's will in all areas of our lives.

For many of us, satan cannot successfully tempt us with drugs, alcohol, criminal activity, or even sexual sin. However, if he can get us out of God's will, our lives are in position for serious enemy attack. Unfortunately, when one area is out of God's will, it throws the other areas out, because we are not in the right place, at the right time, doing the right thing. It is really easier to please people instead, because people-pleasing gives us immediate temporary gratification. Their smile and a pat on the back is all the incentive that we sometimes need. Things appear to look much more peaceful than if we told them how we really feel, what we really want to do, and what we really do not want to do. Is silence really peace? Real peace lies in following the principles of the Word and the direction of the Holy Spirit.

Especially as Christians, many of us consider it earth-shattering if someone disapproves of us in any way. On the flip side of this concept, we feel validated when we are complimented and approved of. Too often, when people are pleased, God is not pleased.

It is emotionally unhealthy for us to depend on the thoughts and beliefs of others to elevate our spirits. In actuality, only what we think of ourselves can be influential to our feelings and emotions. Truly, it is not worth the price when we compromise the will of God for our need for social acceptance from others.

For the most part, the approval or the disapproval of others has nothing to do with us, but reflects their own environmental influences. Some people have been raised in the homes of extremely critical, irrational, and/or addicted parents. It is difficult for a child to try to please an unreasonable parent. Such exposure can later cause the adult to blame themselves when someone disapproves of them and they need constant validation to avoid depression, anxiety, and other emotional disorders. If we identify such a pattern in ourselves, we must take the challenge of appraising our situations realistically and seek ways to combat this area of vulnerability. Then we will be able to hear God's direction for our lives and move forward in the purpose that He has for us.

Sometimes we have a problem determining whether we are hearing the voice of the Lord or of the enemy. There are some key factors that will bring clarity to this dilemma. First of all, is the direction in harmony with the Word of God?

Will the results of your decision cultivate your relationship with the Father? Will it increase Godly character within you? Will it lead to more crucifying of the flesh and radiate more of Christ in you? Is God being put first in this situation? Weigh all of these questions as you seek God's will.

God is waiting for His will to become number one in your life. If you lose the love of the people whom you please by standing for what you believe is God's will, did you ever really have their love? Putting others before Him will cause the covering of God's will to be violated, thus God's plan and purpose will be restrained. If this is the situation in your life today, seek God's plan by His Spirit. Do not bow to the will of the enemy through people. Seek His face. In all of your ways acknowledge God and He will direct your path. Take cover! This is "Where Bondage Ends."

## *Where Bondage Ends*

Like the green to fresh cut grass
The stump to the blowing leaves
Like the red to the sparkling rose
The blue to the calming sea

Like the wave to the endless ocean
The soft beach to the crystallizing sand
Like the wetness is to water
The vegetation to the land

Like the stem to the flower
The colors to the bouquet
Like the water to the parching soil
The potter to the clay

Is God's will in the life of the Christian
Its entrance makes life sweet
If you do not seek passionately His face and His will
Victory will become defeat

For there is a way
That seemeth right to man

Leads to death and destruction
Not in God's plan

Your way may be lawful
But not expedient
God's way, God's timing
Should not go against

If presently you are not in His will
God your path can change right now
Cast your cares upon Him, seek His face
The Shepherd will show you how

Sheep of the great Shepherd
Wherever your life today
Don't blunder around the field causing strife
Let the Omniscient Shepherd lead the way

The wise Shepherd has His own plan for your life
Let His will like clear waters flow
As He leads you into the green pastures of His will
Your territory will surely grow

Defeat what the enemy is determined to steal

Your place in the Master's will

His will welcomes His presence

Where you will find fullness of joy

Jesus is your Savior

Let Him be Lord

THIS IS WHERE BONDAGE ENDS

# "No" – A Beautiful Word

> *"Therefore, you shall love the Lord Your God and Keep His charge, His statutes, His judgments, and His commandments always...Take heed to yourselves, lest your heart be deceived, and you turn aside and serve other gods and worship them, lest the Lord's anger be aroused against you..."*
> (Deuteronomy 11:1, 16-17)

Why do we say, "yes" when we need to say, "no?" What is it that we are really trying to accomplish with a "yes?" Is it God's will or our need to be popular with man? Why is the "yes" so much easier than the "no," even if we really do mean to say, "no?" Sometimes saying "no," even when the Holy Spirit is leading us, feels uncomfortable, and we look upon ourselves as inconsiderate of others. Recently, I had a wake-up call in this area when Joyce Meyers said, "You will never be 'free indeed' as long as you are addicted to the approval of others." That is why saying no is so hard for many Christians. We can be so sensitive to the needs of others that we allow our sensitivity to overpower the will of God. When man's will is different than God's will, we must pursue God's will. It is my experience that when we live according to God's Word, walk in love, and submit to His will, everything and everybody will be in divine order. On the other hand, if we choose to please man instead of God, our actions position everyone involved out of God's will. If you assume the responsibility that God has assigned to someone else, you are really aborting God's plan and enabling the other person. Additionally, what you are supposed to be doing at the time goes undone.

As I continued to ponder on the "why" of not wanting to say no when we mean no, being a Clinician by profession, I first used a clinical approach. For example, I pondered over whether Esau said no to giving up his birthright because he was very hungry or because he was very passive. However, God showed me that it was neither of the two, but instead, it was his lack of faith. Esau said, "What does a birthright mean when I am getting ready to die anyway?" Esau, the grandson of Abraham (Father of Faith), did not have enough faith to believe that God would touch Jacob's heart to feed him without him paying the price of his birthright. Esau, who was a hunter of meats, gave up his birthright in fear of dying of hunger! Have you feared saying no to loved ones, thus being untruthful to them, to avoid risk of rejection, relationship change, love loss, or their withdrawal from your life? Have you resisted saying no to your spouse's abuse because you fear being alone? Do you dance to the beat of your adult children to keep them happy when God has led you to say no to them?

In my personal life and professional field as a licensed Clinical Therapist, I have witnessed people compromising much for love and companionship. Parents compromise their moral or ethical standards to keep their children from leaving home. Women compromise by exposing their bodies to abuse to keep their man in the home. People go along with the crowd and compromise their relationships with God to keep acceptance flowing from family members.

In truth, the measure of love and consistency of love by others is, at many times, considerably unpredictable. Your compromise will not always determine the security of their love. It is ultimately up to you to secure your emotional stability and self-worth through your love for yourself. Instead of compromising yourself as a person for the assurance of people being around you and staying in your life, be content in the state that you are in. Continue to love them, but stand for whom God has made you. Consider the advantages of being alone. Identify and develop the things that you have always wanted to do for yourself. Prepare for your dream career. Always seek God's direction and timing. As you cultivate yourself, you will naturally draw others to you. You will discontinue enabling others with your spirit of pacifying compromise. Most of all, you will develop a relationship with yourself. As you spend time doing things that give you a sense of accomplishment and gratification, you will develop into the only person other than God that can complete you. Allow God to prepare you for your royal assignment without operating in the fear of being alone.

Christianity is all about being followers of Christ and fulfilling the purpose of God in our lives. In order to walk in this priestly assignment, we must realize that when the Holy Spirit's position in a given situation is not yes, "No Is a Beautiful Word." We must have the faith to know that when we are obedient to God's direction, He will handle every other aspect of our situation to His Glory and His Honor.

## *"NO" – A Beautiful Word*

Hated to say "no"
Even when I saw the need
But who the Son sets free
Is free INDEED!

No is sometimes
The answer that is best
Let the Spirit lead you
Pass the test

When God says say "no"
No you must face
Everything else
Will fall into place

But if you say yes
When you need to say no
All will be out of order
Seeds of confusion you will sow

God gives you your unction
Through the Holy Ghost

Got to please God
Cannot always please folks

I know Mama said, "Don't tell me no"
In your ear that voice still rings
But now that you have become men and women
You must put away childish things

Say "no" with courage and you will find
"No" can be gentle – "No" can be kind
When "no" is the order of God's divine plan
It may not always be understood by man

But go forth with "no" in its purity
And God's glory will be revealed through His sovereignty
"NO" can be a beautiful word
When through it the voice of God is heard.

# THE SUBTLENESS OF THE SILENT "YES"

*"A truthful witness saves lives, but a false witness is deceitful."* (Proverbs 14:25)

*"The Lord detests lying lips, but he delights in men who are truthful."* (Proverbs 12:22)

*"Truthful lips endure forever, but a lying tongue lasts only for a moment."* (Proverbs 12:19)

There was a hymn that we used to sing when I was a little girl called "In The Garden." It begins with the line, "I come to the garden alone." Well, guess what? The first man, Adam, was taken to the garden alone by God.

Adam, alone, was given the command by God not to eat of the Tree of Good and Evil. After he was given that command, God gave him a wife, Eve. I don't know whether or not Adam and Eve spent all of their time together. However, I do know that when she ate of the forbidden fruit, Adam was, according to the Bible, with her.

There is no indication that Adam verbally agreed to disobey the command of God. The "yes" to disobedience was silent; "He did eat." Thus, Adam silently responded to the subtleness of the serpent through Eve. Did he remember God's command? Of course he did. Did he understand that it was wrong to eat of the forbidden fruit? Certainly he did. More than likely, he did not know the magnitude of the consequences of his disobedience until it was too late. In other words, he did not realize that God does not make requests – He makes commands.

Surely we can relate to Adam's mistake. Yet, how often do we silently say "yes" to things that we know are wrong? Silence is agreement. So, if we do not stand for right by our actions and/or words, we are taking a position of agreement to the situation at hand. You may remain quiet for the sake of peace. If it is against God's Word and will, it is unrighteous. Without righteousness, there can be no real peace.

Peacemaking is a process of communication, not silence. God's peace is in His Word, and He says, "My peace I leave with you, a peace that the world cannot give, I give to you" (John 14:27). The world represents unrighteousness and darkness in which there is no peace. Do not follow man. Man changes like the weather. Follow God. He changes not. Make a decision to stand in obedience to God and not be a victim to "Subtleness of the Silent Yes."

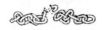

## *The Subtleness of the Silent "Yes"*

As children of the Most High God
We don't take pleasure in unrighteousness
Yet we sometimes do not take a stand either way
And bow to the subtleness of the silent "yes"

Reflect back to Adam and Eve with the serpent
They did not respond with an acceptance address
She listened to the serpent, fruit was appealing, they did eat
Left the world in a mess
Bound by the subtleness of the silent "yes"

We ignore God's righteousness
to please family and friends
As happily they smile bright
Then God shows up in the cool of the day
And exposes the darkness with His light

Our response to unrighteousness should be prayer
Not always verbal confrontation
Yet, at times God directs us to speak the truth in love
– Don't be afraid
It will lead to healing, not condemnation

Love one another enough to expose works of darkness

Through the light of righteousness

Love God enough not to grieve the Holy Spirit

By yielding to the subtleness of the silent "yes"

# FROM PARANOIA TO REST

*"Rest in the Lord and wait patiently for Him; Do not fret because of him who prospers in his way, because of the man who brings wicked schemes to pass. Cease from anger and forsake wrath. Do not fret – it only causes harm."* (Psalm 37:7-8)

*"There remains therefore a rest for the people of God. For he who has entered His rest has himself also ceased from his works as God did from His. Let us therefore be diligent to enter that rest, lest anyone fall according to the same example of disobedience."* (Hebrews 4:9-11)

*"Finally, brethren, whatever things are true, whatever things are noble, whatever things are just, whatever things are pure, whatever things are lovely, whatever things are of good report, if there is any virtue and if there is anything praiseworthy — meditate on these things."* (Philippians 4:8)

Paranoia is a state of unrest. He who enters into God's rest ceases from his own works by displaying obedience. This state of unrest is a form of psychosis indicating a partial or complete withdrawal from reality. It is unreasonable distrust and suspicion. Additionally, it is an exaggerated sense of one's own importance, thinking that others are focusing on you enough to revolve their actions around you. The reality is that others are usually so absorbed with their own issues and situations that focusing their behavior on you is not high on their list of priorities.

If you are on their list to torment, however, pray, focus on the Word, and ignore them. What can they achieve without an audience? Do not choose their agenda over God's rest. The bottom line is that if we believe God's Word and who we are in Him, we will not be tormented by fears of the actions of others. We must not exercise unbelief, but instead, enter God's rest. After accepting Jesus' salvation, it is disobedient not to enter into His rest!

One way that we can avoid paranoia is to think the best concerning one another's actions, even if we do not understand them. Then rest in the Lord. In the natural body, rest allows the muscles that we have broken down to heal and recover. As the body recovers, it is able to handle the increased weight. During sleep, growth hormone levels are at their highest. If proper recovery is not given, the body cannot regenerate. Hard training will break down your muscles and make you weaker.

As we rest, in the natural, all stress is on the object on which we are lying, such as our bed. When we rest in God, we are casting all of our cares upon Him. Even if our paranoia is justified, if the person is against us, we must do as God tells us in Psalm 37:7-9. Rest in the Lord and wait patiently for Him to handle the situation. In this same passage, God tells us not to fret because someone is appearing to prosper in bringing wicked schemes to pass. He tells us not to fret because it is harmful to us. When we fret, we are not committing our way to the Lord. We must wait patiently on God's promise that the evildoers will be cut off, but the meek shall inherit the earth.

As we rest, the muscles of our inner man, our spirit man, will be built up and recover from the cares of life. Restoration and growth will equip us to properly evaluate situations and effectively proceed in our purpose, evangelism, and spiritual warfare.

Just as rest is important for the natural body builders, it is essential for us as we minister to and build up the Body of Christ. You do not have to prove anything, because God will bring forth your righteousness as the light and your justice as the noonday.

Do not let paranoia have you bound. Be delivered "From Paranoia to Rest."

## *From Paranoia to Rest*

I see them over there in that huddle
I know they are talking about me
After all, I'm the only outcast in the group
So who else could their subject be?

I have made all kinds of attempts to fit in
But no matter how I try
They can do the same thing I do and get praised
But me?  I get criticized!

Oh no – now they are laughing
And right in front of my face
That's it!  I'm not good enough
Everyone is against me!
Lord! Get me out of this place!

If this is you, you have reached a self-conscious state
That you really should avoid
I know because I have been there, done that!
Yes, I have been paranoid

You have delusions of persecution,
personalize others' looks, decisions, and acts
You have irrational distrusts and suspicions
Sometime beyond all reason, intellect, or fact

Your thoughts are distorted and turned inward
You are no longer abiding in the vine
Rest in God is interrupted
You must be transformed by the renewing of your mind

Some people, but not ALL, are against you!
Address their problem through prayer – don't stress!
Meditate on who you are in Christ
Be God-conscious
And transform from paranoia to rest!

# NEW GLORY

> *"In Him also we have obtained an inheritance, being predestined according to the purpose of Him who works all things according to the counsel of His will that we who first trusted in Christ should be to the praise of His glory."* (Ephesians 1:11-12)
>
> *"Therefore, I ask that you do not lose heart at my tribulations for you, which is your glory."* (Ephesians 3:13)

Therefore, having been justified by faith, we have peace with God through our Lord Jesus Christ, through whom we also have access by faith into His grace, and rejoice in hope of the glory of God. Not only that, but we also glory in tribulations, knowing that tribulation produces perseverance; and perseverance, character; and character, hope. Now hope does not disappoint, because the love of God has been poured out in our hearts by the Holy Spirit who was given to us (Romans 5:1-5).

Yes, as Christians (believers), we are the righteousness of God, the head and not the tail, above and not beneath. We have to acknowledge, however, that we possess these attributes only because of the nature of God's Spirit within us. Allowing our focus to be on who we are instead of who He is will allow pride to infiltrate our spirits and our situations. When we maintain His attributes in the midst of persecution, His pure and unchanging righteousness is manifested before the eyes of men.

Truly, I was in awe late one night when God exposed me to the revelation that if offense is present, pride is present. If we are offended, pride is involved. What is pride? It is an extremely high opinion of ourselves. So what if we were falsely accused? Jesus never did wrong and He was falsely accused. Can we say that about ourselves? In our flesh, we deserve nothing. Jesus paid the price for us to be accepted in the beloved. Our righteousness is still as filthy rags compared to His righteousness.

Your victory, during times of criticism, will be determined by how you respond to your critic. It is you who has the choice of whether or not to feed your critic's statements with your own negative, distorted thoughts of yourself. It is your emotional reaction that will determine whether or not you will accept the criticism as legitimate and sound. When you are being criticized, analyze accusations to determine if they are unrealistic and irrational. Always keep in mind that, if the criticism is incorrect, there is no reason for you to be upset. When the criticism is justified, remember that you, as a human being, have not yet reached perfection and can be, at times, in error.

Get enough information from your critic to assess what you did to make them unhappy. Try to view the situation from their perspective. If the two of you are able to discuss, rather than attack, mutual respect can enter into the conversation and situation. Find some point of agreement with your critic and build from that point.

> Example: *You're right. I was really in a hurry when you approached me and I may have come across as harsh. But it was not my intent to snap at you.*

Once you reach this point, emotions are likely quieted to the point of listening and discussing. At that point of listening and discussing, you may even be able to disagree agreeably. At that level of communication, each person knows that the other cares enough to listen and enough to want to come into agreement. That knowledge, alone, dulls the hurt and the pain enough for them to pursue reconciliation.

When we get to the point that we can handle persecution by displaying God's attributes, while under attack, we are ready for the next level of displaying His honorable state. That is when we are radiating His glory. Then He can trust us as a bright light that will penetrate the kingdom of darkness. In times of persecution, He strips us of our garments of pride and any attributes that are not like Him so that His glory will be revealed through us. Each time that we come through our trials victoriously, FRESH OIL – VICTORY - NEW GLORY!

## *New Glory*
### *(Isaiah 43:19, Romans 8:18, Isaiah 43:2)*

She came to the well to draw water
And Jesus asked her for a drink
She replied, "Why are you a Jew talking to me, a
Samaritan?"
She did not know what to think

Jesus told her who He was
Described a true worshipper
Offered her a fountain of living water
Then she unclenched her fist
Laid aside her garments of lies and unbelief
Unveiled truth and laid bare at the alter

Have you been stripped of any garments lately?
If not, please wear them loose
For God is yet seeking true worshippers
To worship Him in Spirit and in Truth

Recently I had a fresh stripping of garments
At first I said, "Lord, I get the message
I will gladly step down today
Because Lord, I really want what you want
And, Lord, this really does not feel like your way"

Falsely accused of something?

That I had not done and would never do?

Rejected, laughed at, publicly mocked?

Lord, this could not be you!


God showed me quickly in so many ways

You are exactly where I want you to be

Acknowledge your pain

Show love to your accusers

Lay aside your garments for ME


God said, "Lay aside your garment

of addiction to man's approval

There is fresh oil as you unveil and come bare before Me

Then in a fresh way you will touch My world and speak to

its heart

This present pain is the cost of NEW GLORY"


He said, "Lay aside your hurt and the need to impress

Bring only what is true before ME

Then I will know that your heart and spirit are pure

And I can trust you with NEW GLORY"


Saints of the Most High God

God will continue to perfect you

Lay aside any garments that do not glorify the King
That your worship may be true

Then do as the Woman at the Well
Run and tell others your story
Then they will drop their defenses, seek Jesus, the Christ
And become true worshippers with NEW GLORY

# PERFECT LOVE

*"There is no fear in love; but perfect love casts out fear, because fear involves torment. But he who fears has not been made perfect in love. We love Him because He first loved us. If someone says, 'I love God', and hates his brother, he is a liar; for he who does not love his brother whom he has seen, how can he love God whom he has not seen? And this commandment we have from Him: that he who loves God must love his brother also."* (1 John 4:18-21)

*"But I say to you, love your enemies, bless those who curse you, do good to those who hate you, and pray for those who spitefully use you and persecute you, that you may be sons of your Father in heaven; for He makes His sun rise on the evil and on the good, and sends rain on the just and the unjust. For, if you love those who love you, what reward have you? Do not even the tax collectors do the same?"* (Matthew 5:44-46)

God loves us unconditionally and that is how we must love one another. To love one another is not a request by God, but a commandment from God (I John 3:23). God is Love and He abides in His people. He has overcome the world. Therefore, we have overcoming power within us. If we fear what others are going to feel toward us, do to us, not do to us or for us, say to us or not say to us, we are not walking in perfect love. Perfect love is genuine and only concerned about what it can give, not what it will receive.

When we put conditions and expectations on others, fear sets in. We fear because we are not confident as to how we will respond to our preset requirements not manifesting. There is nothing wrong with having expectations from others. However, their fulfillment of our expectations should not be the determining factor of our level of love for them.

Jesus tells us in Matthew 48 that we shall be perfect, just as our Father in Heaven is perfect. To be perfect means that we must be mature, not easily angered, even when we are disappointed by how we are treated. It takes true maturity to control our feelings of disappointment when we always go the extra mile for others who will not go one foot for us. That is why, whatever we do, we must do it from the heart. Then it will not bother us even if they do not acknowledge what we did. We must protect ourselves by minimizing the level of anger that we conceive into our spirits. Overreacting to irritability and disappointment can be real joy killers. Frequent hostile responses can result in tension headaches and increases in blood pressure. Continuously suppressing our anger, rather than expressing it, can lead to depression. Therefore, the best solution is controlling our feelings to the point that we will not create anger.

Others can upset us only if we allow it. When we allow it, we are allowing the other person(s) to be in control of our temperaments. Anger results from our perception of the event, not in the event itself. We can always interpret an event either negatively or positively. It is our choice whether we respond with outrage, deep hurt, or fervent love.

Even in the covenant of marriage, it is necessary that our love be perfect or mature. We have become one flesh. Yet, we have different natures, different past environmental influences, and different experiences. Prior to the fall of man, Adam and Eve were in perfect harmony with one another and were exposed to no other nature. After their disobedience came the choice between harmony or confusion. With Jesus in the center of our marital relationships, we can have that harmonious love again. Yet, it takes much work, much prayer, and much maturity. Something worth remembering is that God is the only one who will always understand, not our mate. Love unconditionally and believe God for the victory. Do not make the mistake of thinking that your love can change your spouse. Only God's love can change hearts. When you consider these concepts, it will strengthen your ability to love without fear of anger and disappointment.

> *"God has given us the ability to love. He has not given us the spirit of fear, but of power, love, and of a sound mind."* (II Tim. 1:7)

Therefore, follow this love menu:

- If they are warm – love
- If they are cold – love
- If they speak – love
- If they do not speak – love
- If they understand – love
- If they misunderstand – love
- If they tell the truth about you – love
- If they lie about you – love
- When they accept you – love
- When they reject you – love
- When they are right – love
- When they are wrong – love

Do not expect the behavior of others to always harmonize with your personal values. LOVE, LOVE, LOVE! As Co-Pastor, Mary Middleton, advises, "See and don't see. It's really a walk." Pray without ceasing. If your spirit continues to be disturbed, it must be time to speak the truth in love. Ask God what to say, when to say it and how to say it. He will show you the way. FEAR NO MORE!

## Perfect Love
### (I John 4:18)

I was tormented,
Afraid!
How can this be?
I am saved!

Dreading to assemble
With the people I love so dear
Afraid of danger!
Why?
When the God who loves me is near?

For my answer I drew nigh to God
He drew nigh to me
Through His Spirit
Came liberty

He showed me perfect love as unconditional, pure
Innocent, without expectation
Surpasses unpleasant looks, words, deeds
Forgives without hesitation
Looks at the good, ignores the bad
Unless God directs confrontation

Perfect love sees past rejection, rudeness, and partiality

Gives spiritual access to the person's real heart

Reveals that hurting people hurt people

Through perfect love, healing will start


Perfect love, mature love

Give it, receive it

Fear will flee with violent force

Perfect love casts out fear – believe it

I fear no more.

# LOOKS CAN BE DECEIVING

> *"We give no offense in anything, that our ministry may not be blamed. But in all things we commend ourselves as ministers of God: in much patience, in tribulations, in needs, in distresses, in stripes, in imprisonments, in tumults, in labors, in sleeplessness, in fastings; by purity, by knowledge, by longsuffering, by kindness, by the Holy Spirit, by sincere love, by the word of truth, by the power of God, by the armor of righteousness on the right hand and on the left, by honor and dishonor, by evil report and good report, as deceivers and yet true."* (II Corinthians. 6:3-8)

Persistent distrust and groundless suspicion is a friend of the enemy and a subtle enemy of the believer. It stunts our growth in God and cripples our walk with God. Even as Christians, we can misinterpret one another's words, actions, expressions, and motives to the point where we personalize them with negative assumptions. That is why the Bible tells us to think the best of one another. If we do not keep our hearts focused on what the Word says about who we are in Christ, we become vulnerable to satan's fiery darts in the form of negative thinking.

There is an internal critic, the enemy of our souls, to whom we must not respond. If we accept these negative thoughts, rest assured that the responses of others will confirm them. That is when the offense will take the driver's seat.

The poetic message "Looks Can Be Deceiving" was written from an incident that I personally experienced on a previous job. My conclusions regarding this incident were the result of a negative concept that I had unknowingly developed over the years. This negative concept indicated that my worth was determined by my accomplishments. Unfortunately, I had allowed life's experiences and pitfalls to temporarily convince me that, if I achieved, I was okay, and that if I failed at something, I was a failure. The flaw in this silent assumption is that no one always achieves. Can we then respect ourselves when we have not, in our standards or the standards of others, earned our personal worth, happiness, and/or the right to respect ourselves? When we base our worth on our achievement, a failure to achieve will leave us inwardly empty and filled with gloom. Fulfillment based on attainment can also make us vulnerable to depression and a variety of other emotional episodes. In life, we are likely to experience failures that are beyond our control. Thus, we must learn emotional survival skills when we are not in a position to receive accolades, pats on the back, and compliments. Be confident, nevertheless, that regardless of accomplishment, we are accepted in the Beloved, God's workmanship gloriously and wonderfully made. We are the head and not the tail, above and not beneath, because of our position in Christ.

When we look upon ourselves as overcomers, accepted in the Beloved, more than conquerors, we can walk in victory. Instead of personalizing the actions of those around us, we can reassure ourselves that, "If they have a problem with me, they must just have a problem." When we can and are led to do so, we must help them with their problem instead of sulking about how it affected us. Is that because we are flawless? Of course not! It is because we are perfecting, repenting, and maturing daily.

There are times when people really are attacking us, when the suspicions are real. In those times, we should not blame ourselves for the attack, because hurting people hurt people. If someone hurts you, shine the light of the Holy Spirit upon the situation to be sure that you are not in error in any way. If you are, get it straight, repent, and turn. If you are not in error, pray for their hurt and their deliverance. In other words, try the spirit by the Spirit to see if it is of God. Then you will have peace, not offense, and "Looks won't be Deceiving."

> *"Great peace have those who love Your law, And nothing causes them to stumble."* (Psalm 119:165)

## *Looks Can Be Deceiving*

As I tell you this story
You must start believing
That looks truly
Can be deceiving

As I rushed toward her
Papers in hand
She frowned and drew back from me
I did not understand

How she could turn on me this way
She was okay earlier that day
Why would she give me a look that could kill
Just to do my job, I had to be run through the mill?

I was filling in for one of my colleagues
Even if I might have to stay half the night
I would do her job, I would do my job
And I would do it with all of my might

But the look that she gave me hurt so much
That I hung my head and went on my way

No one had ever looked at me like that before
So why her? And why today?

When I shared my hurt with her later
Much to my surprise
She came back to me with an answer
That shocked me and opened my eyes.

She expressed to me
That she did not have the heart
To give me more work
She would do my part

She felt that my load was too heavy
For her to be adding more
She was trying to do what had to be done
and get on out the door

So as it turned out
What I perceived as rejection
Was in reality an act of protection.

## COMPROMISE

*"The Lord God said "It is not good for man to be alone. I will make a helper suitable for him."* (Genesis 2:18)

*"But for Adam no suitable helper was found. So the Lord God caused the man to fall into a deep sleep; and while he was sleeping he took one of man's ribs and closed up the place with flesh. Then the Lord God made a woman from the rib he had taken out of man and he brought her to man. The man said 'This is now bone of my bone and flesh of my flesh, she shall be called woman."* (Genesis 2: 20-23)

According to the New International Version Study Bible "not good for man to be alone." means that "without female companionship and a partner in reproduction, man could not fully realize his humanity." God gave man and woman the assignment to be fruitful and multiply, fill the earth and cultivate it.

Compromise is a message that God gave me during the period leading up to our most recent presidential election.

One of the dynamics of this election was the issue of same-sex marriage. There were Christians around me who were under the deception that they had to compromise their standards and convictions in order to keep their jobs and maintain financial stability.

As I approach this introduction, my focus is not to point the finger at the politicians, the candidates or the political parties. My focus is on the unmarried, the mothers and the fathers. That includes everyone because even you adults who do not yet have children, you are parenting children as they observe your lives. Be ever mindful to make the choices, decisions and path of your life according to the will of God.

Did you know that, according to research, the underlying common cause of homosexuality is an emotional detachment from the same-sex parent? People with homosexual life styles believe that they were born that way. According to the genetic experts, there are no such species as homosexual or gay genes.

Am I saying that all children of single-parent homes become homosexuals? Of course not. They are, however, more at risk. Same-sex attraction can begin with an unhealthy home environment absent of nurturing love and, most of all, absent of one parent. Often the child looks upon the absence of the same-sex parent as rejection. With the absence of relational same-sex love, the child develops a legitimate unmet need. This longing for normal same-sex love and affection too often becomes sexualized during the stage of sexual development.

In the absence of the father, some mothers have a tendency to overcompensate by smothering their sons with love and affection. Sometimes this smothering leads the boy into rejecting the natural love and affection of females and, instead, accepting the unnatural affection of males. Homosexuality is a developmental abnormality that can, in many cases, be prevented.

Single-person parents, through Christ you have the power to prevent this same-sex attraction. Keep your body to yourself until God blesses you with a mate of His choice so that you will have a Christ-centered marriage and home environment. Secondly, take your marriage covenant seriously to avoid separation and/or divorce. Do all that you can to develop a wholesome marriage relationship before God and before your children. Then, God forbid, if your marriage does end in divorce, stay in your child's life to keep him or her from being at risk of longing for an unnatural same-sex relationship. Thus, you will preventively be combating the kingdom of darkness in the area of homosexuality and same-sex marriage – without "Compromise."

## *Compromise*

My heart aches
with excruciating pain
At the devil's lies
As I see the enemy come
With the evilness of his disguise
And I see the body of Christ respond
With compromise.

God says take no thought for tomorrow
What you will eat, drink, or what you will wear.
He is with you and is able to supply all of your needs
He knows all about you
Has counted every strand of your hair
He cares.

In Christ we are no longer tossed to and fro
By the Doctrine of evil men
God has shown us the path of life.
Don't compromise his righteousness for sin
And you will win.

Do not bow down to idols
Now you say "No way, not me" and laugh
But remember that an idol is anything
That we put before God
It is not necessarily a golden calf
Don't provoke God's wrath.

You say you are a saint indeed
That you would not put anyone or anything before God
But would you stand for righteousness
Even if it might cost you your job?

Can you believe that God will bless your life
Even if you take a stand?
That only a woman can be a wife?
And that a husband must be a man?

Seek God for who you should vote for
Don't compromise his righteousness for self gain
For the government is still upon his shoulders
His government, His peace will reign.

If you diligently obey God's voice
His blessing will overtake you

Be led by God's Spirit.
Walk in His ways.
He will not leave you
Nor will He forsake you.

Your enemies will be defeated
Before your very face
Not because of your perfection
But because of your obedience
Because of God's mercy; because of God's grace

Our world is facing challenging times right now
But through our disobedience they could become worse
Because just as God promises His blessings to the obedient
To the disobedient He promises His curse.

Babylon, the source of earthly riches
Her fine linen and pearls will be judged and destroyed
In just one hour
But he who keeps God's work until the end
Over all nations He will give us the power.

God's grace is sufficient.
He is Holy and Pure.

He is all-knowing, He is all wise.

Follow His reign.

Precept upon precept

For a blessed life

Without compromise.

## MISSING THE MARK

*"Brethren, I do not count myself to have apprehended; but one thing I do, forgetting those things which are behind and reaching forward to those things which are ahead, I press toward the mark for the prize of the upward call of God in Christ Jesus."*
(Philippians 3:13, 14)

As I studied the first book of the Bible, it became even more crystal clear to me that God is loving, merciful, and forgiving. When Adam and Eve recognized their nakedness through sin, God made tunics of skin and clothed them. After Cain killed Abel, the Lord declared that if anyone killed Cain, vengeance would be taken of him sevenfold. God set a mark on him so that no one would find him and kill him. God sent him away from his native land, but still allowed him to have a wife and children. Abraham, and later Isaac, lied to Abimelech about Sarah and Rebecca being their sisters, respectively. In spite of the disobedience of Adam and Eve, the lies of Abraham and Isaac, and Cain murdering Abel, God continued to bless them, answer their prayers, and supply their needs. He keeps His promises in spite of our disobedience.

When we do miss the mark, we must not let guilt and shame consume us. Choosing remorse over guilt will lead to conviction and repentance, not guilt and condemnation, and produces hope for future victories. Also, remorse gives us a healthy awareness that we have acted inappropriately towards someone or towards ourselves. This inappropriateness is determined by our own personal standards or belief system. Remorse, unlike guilt, does not imply that "you are" what you "did." It focuses on the behavior, not the individual.

Guilt is usually an overreaction in response to a mistake or wrong deed. When we allow guilt to consume us, our mood declines, our thoughts and actions are self-defeating, our self-esteem is crushed, and we feel powerless. The guilt trip can lead to depression, anxiety, and shame. To avoid guilt, it is necessary for us to combat destructive, self-critical thinking.

There are some questions that we can ask ourselves that can help us appropriately assess our situations:

- Should I spend my thought time on self-persecution or on creative problem-solving to prevent it from happening again?

- Is what happened really that awful or am I blowing it out of proportion?

- Is what I said really wrong or was the other person unable to receive the truth in love?

- Does my making a mistake classify me as a "bad person?"

Before we even entertain the painful emotion of guilt, assess the total situation. Our actions could have been appropriate and the other person's reaction may have been inappropriate. If we assess that we were in error, we should seek to learn a lesson from the situation, ask forgiveness, and move on.

Finally, we must not let guilt lead us to involvement in cover-up activity. Ask God to help you accept criticism in a healthy way and continue pressing for the mark. Above what we have done or have not done, we must remember who we are. When we continually punish ourselves, we are non-productive and we drain ourselves as the guilt cycle intensifies. As we develop a strategy for denouncing the guilt trip, our self-love will return or increase. God has commanded that we love ourselves. We must realize that God is the same yesterday, today, and forever, and that He loves us in spite of, not because of.

God's Word says there is no condemnation for those who are in Christ Jesus. Keep pressing toward the mark of the high calling of God in Christ Jesus. Be obedient to God and no matter how many times you "Miss the Mark," get up, repent, and try again. Because of the powerful, shed blood of Jesus, your sins are not even remembered by God.

> *"For we do not have a High Priest who cannot sympathize with our weaknesses, but was at all points tempted as we are, yet without sin."*
> (Hebrews 4:15)

## *Missing the Mark*

Oh, no! I missed the mark again!
And did not carry out my plan
So will I lie down and accept defeat
Or seek God's face and get back into the heat?

Will I listen to the complaints of man
And crawl into my shell?
Or should I move on with the confidence
That through Christ I can do it well?

Do I focus on the voice of my critics
Whether by phone call, e-mail, or letter?
Or do I ask myself if they were in my shoes
Could they do any better?

Things are quite overwhelming right now
But I will make some improvements
God will show me how

To master the ability to work my plan
In all of my chaos, He will stretch out His hand
And the stepping-stone of missing the mark
Will transform into a beautiful Work of Art.

# 4

# $\mathcal{G}$RACE FOR GODLY RELATIONSHIPS

"*A* *ND NOW, O Israel, what does the Lord your God ask of you but to fear the Lord your God, to walk in all His ways, to love Him, to serve the Lord with all your heart and with all your soul and to observe the Lord's commands and decrees...*" (Deuteronomy 10:12,13)

"Relationships which are not God-ordained are combustible sources of super-satanic entrance and residence into the lives that yield. The forming of these relationships strategically and negatively constructs the destiny of the present generation and generations to come."

*-Beverly Armstrong, Author*

GOD, in His divine love and wisdom, gave us relationships – people with whom we share love, laughter, communication, and fellowship. Yet, we must be ever mindful that He created us to be instruments of His glory that He be glorified and magnified through our lives. Therefore, we must avoid entering into relationships that will not allow us to serve our God.

Relationships are the connection of people by blood, situation, and choice. Examples of "situational relationships" are workplace relationships and in-law relationships. Spouses and friends would be considered "relationships of choice." "Blood relationships" have two categories – natural and divine. Natural blood, of course, is the relationships with our natural blood relatives. Another blood relationship is with those born into the Body of Christ through salvation. Last, but certainly not least, is the relationship that supercedes all others – our relationship with God through the shed Blood of Jesus.

Our relationship with God should be at the center of all other relationships. All relationships of choice should develop by divine choice, divine direction, and divine intervention. If we allow God to guide us in every area of our lives, His presence will manifest in every situation. Therefore, He will ordain our situational relationships also.

God will determine who we will be in relationship with and the depth and length of each relationship.

Certainly, we cannot choose our blood relatives. However, the flow (meaning actions and interactions) associated with these relationships is not exempt of God's domain. If we allow the wants and desires of our relatives to supercede God's Word and His direction, we have made them an idol.

Truly, relationships are important. Ungodly relationships can delay, interrupt, or abort the quiet, peaceable life that God has for us. Godly relationships allow us to be spiritually, emotionally, and physically free for our God-ordained assignments.

# THE GARDEN WITHIN

*"But, speaking the truth in love, may grow up in all things into Him who is the head – Christ – from whom the whole body, joined and knit together by what every joint supplies, according to the effective working by which every part does its share, causes growth of the body for the edifying of itself in love."* (Ephesians 4:15-16)

"The Garden Within" basically focuses on the advantage of quality, honest communication, and speaking the truth in love. As people of God in covenant relationships with one another, we must find a balance between guarding our hearts and releasing what is in our hearts. What makes this balance somewhat difficult is that we are all so uniquely different. For example, we may say something that would offend one person, but would bless another. Humility will restrict the spirit of offense. Pride will feed it. God's Word will destroy it. Forgiveness will cancel it. Communication will keep it from recurring. Our one common ground, the Holy Spirit, will guide us in speaking the truth in love and receiving the truth in love.

As a new Christian, I considered silence to be the Christian way. I wanted to avoid any confrontation and even most discussions. To be hurt and act like you are not, to say that something is good when you really do not mean it, to have a good idea and pretend that the idea which someone else gave is the best thing you have ever heard, to say that you agree with something when you do not, and all such untruths, is to be completely dishonest. Prior to my deliverance, I was guilty of all of the above, and many more. In my effort to be Ms. "Holy-Go-Along-With-Anything," I was really being Ms. "Lying-Lips-Unrighteous-Deceit" and, in being this way, I led myself into anxiety and depression. They are what the Bible refers to as "lying lips," which are an abomination to the Lord, but those who deal truthfully are His delight (Proverbs 12:22).

Proverbs 12 says that he who speaks truth declares righteousness, but a false witness, deceit. When God gives us our ideas, instincts and concepts, they are not to be concealed. Why? Because they impart life. God delivered me from this untruthful tongue and gave me the wisdom to replace it with speaking the truth in love. Sometimes, God is the only one that I share my thoughts with. Other times, I am led to share them with others. There are times when the Holy Spirit leads me to just be quiet. When I do speak to God, others, or myself, I speak the truth, not just what I think people want to hear, but what God leads me to say. Actually, the formal "assumed" name of my ministry is "Truth in Love Ministries." I am so thankful to God for my deliverance in that area. If you are in a bondage of this nature, know that it is not of God.

> *"For the wrath of God is revealed from heaven against all ungodliness and unrighteousness of men, who suppress the truth in unrighteousness because what may be known of God is manifest in them, for God has shown it to them."* (Romans 1:18-19)

Learn to speak the truth in love under the direction of God. When you are not led to reveal truth, do not address the matter. Never replace the truth with a lie. Pray without ceasing. You can always talk to God about everything.

From my own experience, relationships will not develop if communication does not reach a certain level. It will always remain a surface-only relationship if there is minimal truthful communication. Some communications analysts share the concept that there are five levels of communication, ranging from superficial to meaningful. These levels are as follows:

***Level One*** – Superficial, non-conflictive small talk.

Example: *What's going on?*

***Level Two*** – Safe, shallow, non-threatening sharing of information.

Example: *Pretty cold outside, huh?* or *Did you hear about that politician on the news?*

***Level Three*** – Opinions are stated.

Example: *That man is certainly not qualified for the position Pastor Smith just gave him.*

Most people in the body avoid Level Three for fear of conflict. Instead, we should learn how to disagree agreeably. This type of relational communication cultivates "The Garden Within" as we peaceably speak the truth in love. The Word of God tells us that there is wisdom in a multitude of counsel. Through quality communication, we can learn to really know, respect, and understand one another, even if we do not agree.

***Level Four*** – We expose ourselves even more and say what we are feeling.

> Example: *My friend said something last night that really hurt me.*

This level, although it appears we risk having our feelings challenged, can take us to a deeper dimension of loving and being loved by one another. It involves a certain level of confidence in our relationship with the person with whom we are communicating. If a relationship can find comfort at this level of communication, it has the potential of becoming a healthy, meaningful relationship.

***Level Five*** – We reveal our feelings and our needs, the depth of our hearts.

> Example: *I really need to have the confidence that you care about me.*

Communication, at this level, indicates that there are feelings of security in the relationship. This is a quality level of communication at which we can comfortably discuss almost anything and end the conversation in peace and love.

We are comfortably sharing our individuality, indifferences, differences, concerns, and challenges. Truth has penetrated the surface and flowed out of the depth of our hearts.

Fellowship more to get to know one another more. Take off the mask.  Be approachable and sensitive to one another. Value one another's feelings. Receive one another's truth in love. Cultivate "The Garden Within."

## *The Garden Within*
### *(Speaking the Truth in Love)*

I must protect it
For it is who I am
My innermost being
Fragile petals, fragile leaves, fragile soil
Not whom I have chosen to be,
but who God created me to be

Cannot make you love me
Cannot make you be my friend
Cannot make you accept me
But still we can win
Without allowing you to
trample or stampede
On my garden within
So I'll tell you things that you do not know
So my garden can continue to grow

When the tool of your words crush my petals
If your weeds of discord poison my soil
Or if your seeds of confusion enter in
Fallow ground can be softened

There is no need to toil
Or be open to depression
But use the fragrance of expression

Then will you know
If you have caused rain or pain
Whether or not to do it again

God gives us gentle showers from above
It is simply speaking the truth in love
I will know the real you and you the real me
The truth that we know
Will set us free
Communication, Growth, Edification —
Full Bloom.

# MESSAGE IN THE WAVES

> *"I, therefore, the prisoner of the Lord, beseech you to walk worthy of the calling with which you were called, with all lowliness and gentleness, with longsuffering, bearing with one another in love, endeavoring to keep the unity of the Spirit in the bond of peace."*
> (Ephesians 4:1-3)
>
> *"From whom the whole body, joined and knit together by what every joint supplies, according to the effective working by which every part does its share, causes growth of the body for the edifying of itself in love."*
> (Ephesians 4:16)

During one of the wonderful vacations that God blessed us to have, I sat on our patio in front of the ocean and observed the waves. Amazingly, God gave me a message through the waves. It was a message of unity, or the lack of, in the Body of Christ. The big waves joined the little waves and they rode the tide as one. There was no competition within the rolling waters. When they reached the shore, they were powerless, no matter what size they had been before. The wave was no more. The shore represents Jesus, and once the waves (believers) reached Him, they were consumed by His power.

God has a divine purpose for all of our lives. When He fulfills His purpose through us, He is magnified and glorified. Others that our lives touch are blessed, healed, delivered, encouraged, and enlightened through what God, in His divine wisdom, has deposited in us. In Proverbs 18:16, God's Word says our gifts make room for us and bring us before great men. Yet, with all of this divine intervention and manifestation, there is too much competition, jealousy, discouragement, and rejection in the Body of Christ. Instead of coming together as an army against satan, we tend to rejoice in one another's failures. Instead of using our giftings to cultivate and develop others, we isolate and reject those whose giftings have not reached our level of expectation and maturity. Sometimes when we do give constructive input, it is with such a superior approach that they question if the gift that they thought God had deposited in them even exists. On the other hand, we should always reach for excellence in our giftings and have a teachable spirit. None of us have reached perfection and we are still in "the big room" (of improvement) as my Bishop, Bishop Charles Middleton Sr., so tenderly exhorts. He who started the work is able to complete it in you (Philippians 1:6).

Waves are energy from the wind, moving crosswise over the surface of the ocean. The size of the wave is determined by the direction the wind blows over the water, how long the wind blows, and how fast the wind blows. Waves get bigger as they draw more energy from the wind. Constructive wave action can make beaches. As Christians, we must pull together in a constructive way and ride the tides of our lives as one.

If the waves can obey God's will and join the tide as one, why can't we support and promote one another by joining forces? Then we can form a mighty army against the enemy instead of one another. After all, He who commands the winds and waves is within us. Peace — Be Still. Let's learn from the message in the waves. Jesus waits on the shores of our hearts.

## *Message In the Waves*

God speaks to us in so many ways
Sent me a message through His waves
As I look out at the ocean
In the cool of the eve
Revelations in God's waves ...
SURPRISINGLY!
Waves rolling high, but did not portray strife
Displayed God's pattern for Christian life

As one wave rolled up high
It seemed like the next
Said, "I will rise even higher
Whatever the test"

As we see waves of righteousness roll high
Should not settle for average
Reach for the sky
In spreading God's glory, in telling His story

When shorter, less powerful waves
would come
Waves immediately joined it

They rode the tide as one
Tightly, jointly fit together
Did not separate – whatever the weather
Strong waves bore the infirmities of the weak
No vainglory did they seek

Jesus, Himself, represents the shore
As the waves approach Him
Tide no more
Wave no more

As we die to self, to our identity
Me in Christ – Christ In Me
No confusion, no strife,
No tide, no current
The Glory!

# I DO! OR DO I?

> *"Do not be unequally yoked together with unbelievers. For what fellowship has righteousness with lawlessness? And what communion has light with darkness? And what accord has Christ with Belial? Or what part has a believer with an unbeliever? And what agreement has the temple of God with idols? For you are the temple of the living God ..."* (II Corinthians 6:14-16)

II Corinthians 6:16 goes on to tell us why we cannot be in covenant relationship with someone who is walking according to the kingdom of darkness:

> *"I will dwell in them and walk among them. I will be their God, and they shall be My people."* Therefore, *"Come out from among them, and be separate, says the Lord. Do not touch what is unclean, and I will receive you."* (II Corinthians 6:16)

The decisions and choices that we make in our lives affect the quality, standard, direction, and success of not only our lives, but also the lives of generations following. When you are seeking God for a husband or wife, do not let satan's ideas deceive you. The person God will choose for you will have much more than the belief that there *is a God.* To "believe in" means to "walk with, depend on, trust in, and rely on." If a person is not committed to living according to the Word of God, there is a strong probability that he or she does not believe in God. When someone believes that God has paid the price for sin, they will love Him and want to obey Him. Of course, we all miss the mark at times. Yet, for the believer, unrighteousness will not be the standard, pattern, or norm, for, according to Matthew 5:6, "Blessed are those who hunger and thirst after righteousness. For they shall be filled." God wants His married believers to be yoked together with His attributes so that they can be joined together in harmony.

After your decision to accept Jesus Christ, marriage is the most important decision that you will make. "For this reason a man will leave his father and mother and be united to his wife they will become one flesh" (Genesis 2:24). Be extremely careful with whom you decided to become one flesh. Just as God wants you to be evenly yoked, the enemy is on assignment to ensure that you are *unevenly* yoked. Satan wants to be confident that the yoke of the kingdom of darkness will be attached to your life and the lives of generations following.

Do not believe satan's lie that, because the unsaved person was raised up in the church as a child and attends church occasionally, you can change them after marriage. In the premarital relationship, he or she seeks to please you. Therefore, if he or she is not walking with God before marriage, there is a high possibility that they will not change after the ceremony. If the person is not in Christ, they are as determined to change you as you are to change them.

When you are not equally yoked, you open your life to not only strife and conflict, but also continuous interruption of your fellowship with God. Since the two of you are one, you are joined to two different kingdoms. You are vulnerable to idolatry because you are in a position to choose your mate's word over God's Word. When you are receiving commands from both kingdoms, which kingdom will you choose?

Well, he or she may say that they do not believe in God, but is a good-hearted person of moral value. First of all, if they do not believe in God, they are a fool (Psalm 53). Additionally, if the foundation of their moral values is not the Bible, what is the source?

If God is your Father, He will not leave you in the dark. When a person professes to be a Christian, but displays behaviors that are contrary to the Word of God, do not ignore these behaviors. Do not be so busy listening to what they say that you ignore what they do. In all of your ways acknowledge God and He will direct your path (Proverbs 3:6). Marry the person that God leads you to marry the first time so that you can have an "until death do we part" relationship. If God's direction is revealing warnings concerning your marriage to this person, acknowledge Him by asking Him, "I Do! Or Do I?"

# *I Do! Or Do I?*

I'm getting married!
Are you sure?
Has God ordained this union?
Are your decisions pure?

Have you opened up your heart
to recognize His lead?
Or are you just concentrating
On what you want and think you need?

Have you told God that as much
As you think you want this man
That you don't want this marriage
If it is not in His plan?

Are you marrying because
you've committed fornication
And you're trying to make it right?
Don't forsake God's will for a lifetime
For the pleasure of one night
Just repent, turn, walk in the light.

Are you evenly yoked with this person?
Don't say "yes" just because you're both saved
What you want in life, what he wants in life,
Your commitments; are they the same?

Has he told you the secrets of his heart?
Have you told him yours?
If you have unknown separate agendas
Misery is in store.

You may think that life is passing you by
That this may be your last chance
But if God's hand is not upon it
It's just a ceremony, a song, and a dance

Is this person independent
Carrying his own load?
Can he assume your livelihood
If you cannot up the road?

Are you ready to settle for
the lifestyle he can provide?
If two incomes are reduced to one,
can you accept your new lifestyle in stride?

If you have children, does he love them
And not just at their present age?
But will he still be committed to them
When they reach the more challenging stage?

Will he join you
in your commitment to them?
Or complain because it interferes
with your commitment to him?

Is God giving you warnings about him
That you're trying to ignore?
He will not leave you in the dark
When you've chosen Him as Lord

If He's giving you warnings, listen
To what He has to say
Don't enter into a lifetime of grief
In exchange for a wedding day

Do not abort God's plan
Whatever you may do
Stay open to God; listen, pray
Be sure that he is God's man for you

By now you are thinking …
Love is what counts
Not all this chitter chatter
You're right – if it's ordained by God
Nothing else matters.

## AND THEN, BOAZ

> *"If then you were raised with Christ, seek those things which are above, where Christ is, sitting at the right hand of God. Set your mind on things above, not on things on the earth."* (Colossians 3:1-2)
>
> *"And you are complete in Him, who is the head of all principality and power."* (Colossians 2:10)
>
> *"He who finds a wife finds a good thing and obtains favor from the Lord."* (Proverbs 18:22)

When Naomi decided that she wanted her two daughters-in-law to turn back and return to their families, it is obvious that the journey had become tedious. Even as bitter as Naomi was about the losses of her husband and sons, she was determined to continue the journey alone. Ruth clung to Naomi and Naomi's God, confessing that only God or death would separate her from Naomi. She did not even seem concerned that she was without husband and children.

Ruth had been exposed to the idolatry in her paganistic homeland. After she recognized this and came into a relationship with Naomi's God, the true and living God, she did not want to turn back. She realized that she was now a widow and that she was eligible to remarry. Yet, she gave priority to her ultimate purpose. Her number one goal was to commit her life to serving her God.

It was apparent that Ruth had been a wonderful wife and daughter-in-law. After reaching Bethlehem, her focus was providing for Naomi. Ruth was obedient to Naomi and carried herself as a lady in front of everyone. She did not run after the young men and disrespect herself. Thus, she remained pure for Boaz, as she followed God's lead.

Boaz assumed the role of a true man of God. He provided covering for Ruth from the first day that she entered his field. Ruth followed Naomi's direction and slept at Boaz' feet, but continued to carry herself as a lady. Naomi advised Ruth that Boaz would then take the lead, and he did. The closest relative would lose his own inheritance if he bought Naomi and Ruth's field. This released Boaz to buy it and take Ruth for his bride.

Pursue God's direction for your life. Delight yourself in the Lord and He will give you the desires of your heart. In all your ways acknowledge God and He shall direct your path (Proverbs 3:6). Stay open to God and be content in your present circumstances. Maintain a loving, teachable spirit.

Be a slave to God's will. Keep yourself pure. Make God the center of your life.

Dwelling on, or being consumed with the idea of having a husband is like watching a pot boil. It seems to take forever; and, women, the Bible says the man will find you. Get involved with enhancing your quality of life and fulfilling your royal assignment. Continuously spend intimate time with God in prayer and in His Word.

In my own experience, I did not concentrate on getting a husband. As a matter of fact, my mind was far from that. Truly, I was content in my singleness with Christ as my husbandman, enjoying my peace of mind and my new commitment to God. My future husband and I became friends and I actually cried when I started feeling like I was falling in love with him. Fear entered in because I figured that anyone who had the ability to make me happy also had the ability to hurt me. God developed our relationship into what He wanted it to be.

AND THEN, BOAZ! AND THEN, CHARLES!

## *And Then, Boaz!*

Don't send me back to Moab, Naomi
Although our husbands have died
Because, Naomi, I have fallen in love with your God
In Moab, I won't survive

Don't send me back to Moab, Naomi
The gods they serve there are false
I now love the true and living God
Now, my life has a true cause

Don't make me return to my mother's house
Take me to Bethlehem with you
It doesn't matter that
you can't provide me a husband
For the God we serve is true
But the god of Moab is Chemosh
To bow to him will lead me to doom

I don't care if I don't have a husband
Wherever you lodge I will lodge
Your people will be my people
I am committed to your God

Don't make me leave with Orpha
Where you die, I will die
For your God is now my God
He will fit me for the sky


So let's move forth to Bethlehem, Naomi
I will not compromise
My relationship with the Creator of Heaven and Earth
The All-knowing and All-wise
I will never bow down to idol gods again
The King of Kings is my Husbandman


AND THEN, BOAZ!

# SLAVERY: THE ESSENCE OF SUBMISSION

> *"For the wicked shall not rule the godly,
> lest the godly be forced to do wrong."*
> (Psalm 125:3, Living Bible)

Godly submission is to come under or be in harmony with the authority and mission of God. The meaning of submission in marriage has been greatly misunderstood and is often a key factor in marriage conflicts and divorce.

For the husband and wife, the first order of submission is to the absolute authority, God. James 4:7 says, " … submit to God. Resist the devil and he will flee from you." As we submit to God's thoughts and ways, we combat all other thoughts and ways. What we submit to should line up with the heart of God, drawing us near to Him and moving us away from the kingdom of darkness.

Yes, women should obey their husbands, but not when his request is against God's Word and will. God will judge us as individuals, and He pardons us individually. The covenant of marriage cannot shield the partner who displays and inflicts harmful behavior on the other, nor can the covenant defend the one who submits to this wickedness.

Although females lost their gender equality by yielding to sin, it was recovered through relationship with God through Jesus Christ. Obedience is not according to gender, but according to God's authority, according to His Word. Galatians 3:28 tells us that there is neither male nor female, for are all one in Christ Jesus. Do not allow evil men to use obedience scriptures to influence you to submit to their physical, verbal, or emotional abuse. God is holding you responsible to protect your heart, mind, body, and spirit from the bondage of the evil one.

Eve yielded to the serpent's word above God's Word and Adam decided to obey Eve instead of God. Whose words are you bowing to? Are you submitting to someone who God does not want to control you? Are you under the control of an enemy of God?

If your husband is submitted to God, submitting to him is a delight. I am speaking from experience. There is no bondage in submission when husband and wife are committed to one another and are slaves to the will and Word of God.

Do not allow a spouse to blame you for his violence, abuse, and wickedness. If you take a stand in the strength of God, it may allow him to recognize his lack of love and self-control. If he tries to enforce submission that is against the authority of God, he is on assignment by satan to abort your spiritual maturity and that of your children.

Submit one to another in the fear and reverence of God, being slaves to the authority of God. Slavery to God is the essence and the beauty of submission. The Holy One of Israel is the Master.

## *Slavery, the Essence of Submission*

The dew from the kiss is not quite as wet
The heart now skips one beat instead of two
Some of the stars in your eyes have faded
Quality love time has become the exception
Instead of the rule

Enthusiasm is losing its luster
Communication has lost some of its glow
Sweet tones of praises have been hushed
By chilled complaints as hazardous
As fresh fallen snow

"Where," says forever love,
"do I go from here?
Surely this is the love of my life
Why am I now flooded with fear?"

"I am glad you asked," said the Lord of Hosts
Truly I have been wanting to give you this tip
That, as the commitment by the slave to his Master,
Such is the essence of submission in relationship"

"Some people may understand this theory
Yet relationships are still in disaster
Because commonly what is not understood
Is that I, God, not their spouse, am the Master"

The slave seeks his master's pleasure and will
Above all other consideration
Agrees to submit to the master in all ways
No boundaries of place, time, or situation

The slave's actions and speech express
Attitudes and habits of his master's traditions
The slave constantly seeks to learn
how to please his master better
Gracefully accepting chastisement or criticism

God says, "It is Me that you must serve
My ways, my Word above all else
Pleasing me must be number one
But to do that, you MUST die to self"

He says, "Study my Word
To learn more about me
No relationship can be truly
Successful without me"

God ordained the husband as head
to be the final authority
When we cannot agree
But headship is not a position of superiority
But of responsibility

Sir, you did not speak up
When Eve listened to the serpent
Thus came the fall of man
Therefore, Sir, God is now holding you responsible
For carrying out His plan

Submission is not mindless obedience
Let the true description give both spouses a lift
Submission is a NATURAL response
To loving, Godly leadership

Submission is not surrender
It is an attitude of the heart
Surrender is not yielding under force
Force on anything makes it crumble and part

God does not force anyone to follow Him
So why should we force one another?

If the first rule in our relationship is love
We will prefer one another to the other

Husbands, you must love your wives
As you do yourselves
And as Christ loves His Church
You will not expect her to submit to evil
If you are a slave to God's will and God's Word
For if Sapphira had not submitted
To Annanias' lie
She would have told the truth
Would have lived instead of died

Submit first to God, the first Husbandman
Then you will understand
That, as you are both modeling sacrificial love
You can submit to one another
And walk hand in hand

Wives, you can move your man
More by smiling than barking an order
God made you as his helpmate
For each to compliment the other
Melt his stern look with a gentle kiss
Inspire him by telling him how wonderful he is

For relationships often begin to deteriorate
When one wants their opinions to dominate

God says, "One day you two will stand
before me one by one
To give account of your life
Certainly, if the slave can serve the master
who has him bound
You, whom I have set free,
can serve Me as husband and wife"

As I close this message,
I have one more thing to say
That I can testify after going on 23 years
that it works when you do it God's way
Of course, we have our ups and downs,
but submission has been
a pleasure, not a disaster
It feels good, it feels right
It is a natural response of the heart
When you're both submitted to THE MASTER.

# WOMEN IN AUTHORITY, UNDER AUTHORITY

> *"Therefore submit yourselves to every ordinance of man for the Lord's sake, whether to the king as supreme, or to governors, as to those who are sent by him for the punishment of evildoers and for the praise of those who do good. For this is the will of God, that, by doing good, you may put to silence the ignorance of foolish men – as free, yet not using liberty as a cloak for vice, but as bondservants of God. Honor all people. Love the brotherhood. Fear God. Honor the king."* (1 Peter 2:13-17)

The whole issue of authority in our culture is, in general, misunderstood. Authority is defined as the right or power to enforce laws. Jesus, the Ruler of the Nation, rose from the dead with all power in His hands. Therefore, He has absolute authority. Our level of authority is only appropriately measured by how humble we are and by the level of our submission to Him. If our submission to Him is not genuine, we cannot expect Him to trust us with authority. Real submission requires a serving spirit, being humble, meek, patient, selfless, and a giver.

Even letting people use you is in order if it is for the purpose of God. Sometimes when people use you it is not out of disrespect. It is because you possess something that they need to get them where they need to go. They cannot become who they need to become without you being available to them.

When reflecting on "Women in Authority Under Authority," I am reminded of Deborah, the Prophetess, Wife, and Judge of Israel (Judges 4). What a combination of roles of authority and submission. Deborah handled the roles well. It was obvious that, above all else, she was committed to the authority of God's plan and purpose. Responding to God's command to take an army to Mt. Tabor, she sent for Barak and summoned him to go. Yet, she submitted to the designated authority of the venture by adhering to Barak's request for her to go with him. It is obvious that Deborah had already coordinated this with her husband, Lapidoth, because she confidently agreed immediately. In obedience to God, the Commander of it all, she proceeded to carry out His plan, and on the day of the battle told Barak to get up and follow the Lord. When the battle was won, Deborah and Barak praised the Lord for the avenging of Israel. Deborah supported the plan of her God, respected the authority of her husband and God's authorized campaign leader, Barak. She was truly a woman "In Authority Under Authority."

## *Women in Authority, Under Authority*

Women in authority, under authority
What a challenging phrase
But is there anything too hard for God
When we seek His face?
As we approach the challenge
With great expectancy
As we follow God's assignment
to be women in authority
And yet under authority

Let's take charge
of the tasks God assigns to our hands
And yet humbly submit to His will
Obey the ones who have rule over us
Teach, preach His Word, and yet – be still
Some of us may say, "I don't teach, preach, or lead
Even on my job, I'm not in authority"
But you're a queen in God's royal priesthood
You must lead in spreading His glory, you see

Let's take charge of our royal assignments
Without murmur or dispute

Prepare mind, body, and spirit for warfare
With God's whole armor on, we can still be cute

Let's learn to be slow to speak, swift to hear
Whether your role is professional, mother, or wife
Let us think the best of one another
Exemplify that quiet and peaceable life
Let us rise, ladies, to the occasion
In whatever God wants us to do
But be led by the Holy Spirit
Do not be led by you

Let us tread upon the serpent
As the enemy we defeat
But let's do it with a heart that is full of love
In a spirit that is oh, so sweet

For we are not our own, we've been bought with a price
We are under the authority of Jesus, the Christ
The humblest, most obedient servant of all
Let us be like Him as we answer God's call

Women in authority, under authority
Let's die to self and give birth

Delivered by *Grace*

As the divine will of God, the divine plan of God
Flows through us and throughout the earth.

# WIVES OF THE GREAT HIGH PRIEST

*"For your Maker is your husband. The Lord of Hosts is His name. And your Redeemer is the Holy One of Israel. He is called the God of the whole earth. For the LORD has called you. Like a woman forsaken and grieved in spirit, Like a youthful wife when you were refused, says your God."* (Isaiah 54:5-6)

*"For we do not have a High Priest who cannot sympathize with our weakness, but was in all point tempted as we are, yet without sin."* (Hebrews 4:15)

The poetic message, "Wives of the Great High Priest," was especially written to minister to single sisters within and without the Body of Christ. However, this message reminds all followers of Christ of our royal assignments. For we are all a royal priesthood and a holy nation.

During my lifetime, I have been both "single saved" and "married saved." In neither of those situations was I, or am I now, perfect. On, the other hand, I am a witness that, by God's grace, years of holy abstinence can be maintained with joy. When you become a slave to the will of God, there is never a time when you have nothing to do. My experience is that one of the secrets to this single abstinence is recognizing that Jesus is our husbandman. He has royal assignments on which our energies should be focused. Singleness can provide you opportunity to spend intimate time with your husbandman in worship and in His Word in addition to all of your other responsibilities, activities, and recreation. Personally, whenever I would start feeling lonely or sad as a single person, I would check out a good revival, workshop, or Spirit-filled concert. Then I would be so excited and revived by the experience that I would forget about the loneliness. A good movie, a good ball game, a vacation, and even rest can all be sources of restoration.

Review your royal assignment "Wives of the Great High Priest" – " … that you may proclaim the praises of Him who called you out of darkness into His marvelous light; who once were not a people but are now the people of God, who had not obtained mercy but now have obtained mercy." The Great High Priest wants you refreshed as His Kingdom awaits your servanthood.

## *Wives of the Great High Priest*

Sisters, a salute to you
Wives of the Great High Priest
Wives of He who called you unto Himself
As you for His high calling reach

Although the High Priest is your husbandman
It gets lonesome in the earthly sphere
But be content in your present state
Draw nigh unto Him while He is near

As He prepares you for
your second husbandman
Work in His kingdom
Do all that you can
Spread His glory, tend His sheep
Feast on His Word
His pastures keep

He has prepared the table for you
Drink of His pasture, eat of His fruit
Nurture His harvest, cultivate His field
Teach the newborn, help the wounded to heal

Salute to you, wives of the great High Priest
Know that your calling is high
But your affectionate husbandman
Is fitting you for the sky

Take care of your temple
With the Holy Ghost in it
Any battle you have
The High Priest will help you win it

While He prepares you
Surrender to His love
Let Him hold your hand
Get direction from above

Let Him massage your feet in His Holy Word
As in it you walk while His voice is heard
Let Him whisper gently in your ear
As He tells you there is nothing to fear

Bow before Him in His majesty
Submit to the intimacy of His face
Bathe in the oil of His holiness
Wait on Him – you're in a good place...

# 5

# $\mathcal{G}$RACE FOR A GODLY TEMPLE

*"THOSE CONTROLLED BY the sinful nature cannot please God. You, however, are controlled not by the sinful nature, but by the Spirit if the Spirit of God lives within you. And if anyone does not have the Spirit of Christ, he does not belong to Christ." (Romans 8:8-9 NIV)*

The Holy Spirit in the life of the believer is more than powerful enough to reign through any attack, addiction, or bondage of the mind, body, and spirit. With the suffering of bloodshed, torment, and death, Jesus paid the price for us to be physically, emotionally, and spiritually free.

Power of relational, sexual, emotional, and drug-related bondages are no match to the power of the Blood of

Jesus – the sinless, sacrificial Lamb of God. To believe that you are a servant to sin and have no victory over the flesh is to say that Jesus' death was in vain and that His redeeming Blood is of no effect.

> *"Therefore, prepare your minds for action; be self-controlled; set your hope fully on the grace to be given you when Jesus Christ is revealed. As obedient children, do not conform to the evil desires you had when you lived in ignorance."* (I Peter 1:13 – 14 NIV Study Bible)

# YOUR BODY, GOD'S TEMPLE

> *"Flee sexual immorality. Every sin that a man does is outside the body, but he who commits sexual immorality sins against his own body."* (I Corinthians 6:18)

Just imagine one young man and one young lady preordained for one another, both determined to keep their bodies pure, waiting to find one another, each waiting to bless one another on their wedding night with their gift of sexual purity. Sexual abstinence is the only acceptable sexual behavior, before God, for the unmarried.

God's plan for intimacy is between male and female in the confines of the marriage covenant. He designed sexual intimacy for the loving, one-flesh covenant relationship. Consequently, outside of such a relationship, the sexual partners are bound in flesh, but not in spirit. Yet, this bond is powerfully and significantly developed. This powerful emotional, psychological, physical, and spiritual link is so strong that, for a moment, the two people become one.

When one partner ends the relationship without the consent of the other, the non-consenting partner is left feeling emotionally and mentally crushed. Reports identify the following:

- According to The Medical Tribune: Sexual relationships are often leading risk factors for adolescent depression and suicide.

- Sexually active single women are nearly four times more likely to be receiving psychiatric care than those who are not.

- For unmarried, live-in women, the depression rates are three times higher than those of married women.

Research still continues on the theory that the hormone oxytorin is released in both partners during sexual orgasms, which intensifies attachment between the partners that grows with each sexual encounter. Not only can this be the beginning of emotional problems, but also can change the God-ordained direction of your life. You have been bought with a price! True love waits! "Your Body" really is "God's Temple."

## *Your Body, God's Temple*

Hear Ye, Hear Ye, – You are not your own
Now that you are in Christ
Your body is the temple of the Holy Ghost
Jesus has paid the price.

Sexual immorality is a different kind of sin
Some in darkness use it as a hobby
But the Word shows we who are now in the light
That this sin is against our own body

So you might think that you can commit it and quit it
But intimacy carries your emotions with it
It does not end with the intimate night passed
The inner soul ties will last and last

Until true repentance
Comes in like a flood
Then there is no condemnation
It is under the Blood

You must no longer defile the temple
It has God's glory within
That you must spread to the souls that He draws
Through you, them He will win

For you are now one Spirit with Him
You are now His precious gem
Do not yield your body to the lusts of man
But to the power of the Blood of the Lamb.

## INTIMACY

> *"I beseech you therefore, brethren, by the mercies of God, that you present your bodies a living sacrifice, holy, acceptable to God, which is your reasonable service. And do not be conformed to this world, but be transformed by the renewing of your mind, that you may prove what is that good and acceptable and perfect will of God."* (Romans 12:1-2)

When you do not do things God's way, they become a big mess. Abram agreed to Sarai's request to go in to Hagar so that he would not be childless, when God had already promised him a child through Sarai. Sarai, however, became impatient, gave Hagar to her husband, and Hagar conceived. Abram and Hagar were not married – Hagar was his wife's maidservant. Well, it may have been okay if the action had stopped there. But sin never stops in one spot. It infects all around it. Ideally, Abram would have a child and he and Sarai would raise the child and live happily ever after while Hagar continued to be her maidservant. That even sounds like a fairytale. It sounds good, but it is not realistic. It is not realistic because we're talking about human beings, intimacy without covenant love relationships, emotions, feelings, and sin. So, what happens? When Hagar got pregnant, she hated Sarai. Here she is carrying Abram's child, and all of his love and affections are going to Sarai because they are in a covenant relationship. Abram and Hagar were in a convenience relationship, fulfilling Sarai's sinful request that she made in response to her doubt and unbelief in what God said. So here comes more confusion. Abram told Sarai to do whatever she pleased to Hagar, Sarai treated her harshly, and Hagar fled from her presence.

God always intervenes lovingly, even when we don't deserve it. God dispatched one of His angels, who prophesied to her and told her to go back to her mistress' house, and gave her God's name for her son, Ishmael. She called unto the Lord as the God who sees. God is so merciful that, even in our mess, He will recognize our affliction and intervene.

Intimacy outside of a covenant, married love has many negative consequences. Protect the generations following, keeping in mind that God's way is the best way.

## *Intimacy*

Cannot get him out of my system
I have tried and it just will not work
He has deceived me, robbed me, made me bleed
Proven beyond all doubt
That he is a jerk

Don't even like him
But I can't leave him alone
What's wrong with me – I don't understand
Saved, sanctified, Spirit-filled
But cannot let go of this man

So tell me, what is it?
What do I lack?
Bound in mind, body, and spirit
By someone who has used my best
And has not looked back

Intimacy was intended for covenant love
Penetration connects and forms an emotional bond
Part of him is now part of you
Even when he is not around

When intimacy is over
Even if he does not come back
Three to four hundred million of his sperm
Have entered your reproductive tract
You two are still connected
Even after he is gone
Up to a week, his sperm is alive in you
You two still have it going on

Physically, he may be in a different part of the world
You two may now be rivals
But in you his semen's alkaline fluids
Are working to prolong sperm survival

Emotionally, you have put your trust in him
So you are vulnerable to emotional distress
You feel confused, violated, and all alone
Feelings exposed, emotions exposed, uncommitted
But you have functioned as one flesh

You have let God down and you are sorry
But your body is yearning for more, without remorse
At this point, you must repent and turn around
And take a stand that before marriage, no intercourse

Your body is the temple of the Holy Ghost
You must present it as a living sacrifice
Your body is no longer your own
Jesus' blood has paid the price.

# EMOTIONAL HEALING

*"But you are a chosen generation, a royal priesthood, a holy nation. His own special people, that you may proclaim the praises of Him who called you out of darkness into His marvelous light; who once were not a people but are now the people of God, who had not obtained mercy but now have obtained mercy."* (1 Peter 2:9-10)

*"For where envy and self-seeking exist, confusion and every evil thing are there. But the wisdom from above is first pure, then peaceable, gentle, willing to yield, full of mercy and good fruits, without partiality and without hypocrisy. Now the fruit of righteousness is sown in peace by those who make peace."* (James 3:16-18)

*"Beware lest anyone cheat you through philosophy and empty deceit, according to the tradition of men, according to the basic principles in this world and not according to Christ."* (Colossians 2:8)

*"That we should no longer be children, tossed to and fro and carried about with every wind of doctrine, by the trickery of men, in the cunning craftiness of deceitful plotting, but, speaking the truth in love ..."* (Ephesians 4:14-15)

*"And you are complete in Him who is the head of all principality and power."* (Colossians 2:10)

Emotional abuse is behavior intended to have power over another through tactics such as humiliation, intimidation, guilt, fear, and bullying. It methodically attacks the victim's self-confidence, sense of self-worth, and the validity of a person's self-concept and insight. This is accomplished through insults, implications, condemnation, and allegations that, if allowed, lower the victim's self-esteem to the point that they can no longer realistically assess what is happening to them.

Some categories of emotional abuse are as follows:

- The offender makes unreasonable demands that you spend all of your time attending to his or her needs. Whatever time you give is never enough and you are continually criticized.

- The offender uses a parent-child form of communication that is inappropriate for healthy adult relationships, often used under disguise of helping. Instead, they are designed to put down and control.

- The offender disqualifies any ideas, perspectives, or thoughts of the other person

- The offender attempts to control the actions of others to get what they want.

- The offender dwells on vulnerable areas such as children, values, compassion, and guilt to get what they want.

- The offender distorts your reactions to things by saying, "You're too sensitive," or "That should not bother you."

- The offender attempts to blow your weaknesses out of proportion to lower your self-confidence and self-worth.

If you are continually entertaining emotional abuse, quit your idolatry. God has shown you the path of life through His Word and His Spirit. In His presence, there is fullness of joy. At His right hand, there are pleasures forevermore (Psalm 16:11). So why should you allow the confusion of man to interrupt the peace of God?

Anyone or anything that you value in a way that you put them before the love and trust that should be indebted to your God is an idol. God wants us to live in reverence of Him.

He does not want us to fear what men will do to us when we do not obey them. To please God, we must have faith, not fear of man. Our God has overcome this world and has all power in His hand. As long as we are walking in His will, He will protect us. But we have to trust Him.

As Christians, we often like to avoid confrontation to retain peace. Speaking the truth in love is an appropriate response to conflict. Sometimes, when we remain quiet, we are aiding the person in selfishness and irresponsibility. Let the Word of God direct your path, not the values of others. If you stand for righteousness, you might win them over for the Lord. However, if you bow to their tactics of manipulation, how will they see your God's power in you? Who has first place in your heart? Who do you trust, your abuser or God? This person is on assignment to remove peace, joy, and unselfish love from your life, to drain you emotionally and abort God's purpose.

Don't bow down to emotional abuse or the emotional abuser. The Son has set you free, and, through Him, you are free indeed.

## *Emotional Healing*

Physical wounds are inflicted suddenly
The puncture comes swift, deep, sure
Skin broken, bleeding, pain, you know you're hurt
You seek the right process for the cure

You see the bloody instruments
Clean the wound, apply anti-infection
Wrap it in sterile bandages
Shield it for environmental protection

The injury is obvious
Treatment soon starts
The body yields to the process
No real trauma to the heart

Emotional wounds develop slowly
They are deep before their existence shows a sign
They puncture your heart and spirit
Cause trauma to your mind

They always come from a vessel you love
From someone close in heart

Who strategically knows the spots to inflict
Your life is in turmoil, anxiety, pain, and stress
WHERE did it all start?

You know that you have been attacked
When someone curses you out,
puts you down, calls you names
You know when it starts
You know when it stops
You do not have to play guessing games

But the dominator gently, but constantly,
manipulates your mind
Under the pretense of love and care
You continually place the emotional wounds in the
unconscious with an emotional scab
To cover the traumatic pain that is there

Consistently, your feelings are not understood
Your needs are not considered, only theirs
You're made to feel guilty without rational facts
By someone who supposedly cares

You walk on eggshells not to upset them
They never give you the courtesy
of listening to you
You're expected to do things
that you find unpleasant and humiliating
Yet, they find fault no matter what you do

Your concerns are labeled as
unimportant overreactions
Who are you to have valid insight?
Yet, their foolish talking they consider wise
Recognize their ignorance
And that you have the mind of Christ

They try to abort your other relationships
To close all outside doors
By belittling other people in your life
Who might give you emotional support

Relations with others,
the dominator constantly attacks
If he or she is not the center,
Then, sister, you must be off track

Love is what you do
Not what you say
Love is kind, does not envy,
behave rudely, nor seek its own
It is the image of God's face

Do not be tossed to and fro
Be renewed in the spirit of your mind
Or you will be alienated from the life God has for you
The trickery of men will make you blind

Jesus was wounded for our transgressions
Christ made you alive
To do the will of God is wise and right
Awake you who sleep! Arise from the dead!
Christ will give you light!

# FREEDOM TO BE – "YOU"

> *"Being confident of this very thing, He who begun a good work in you is able to complete it until the day of Jesus Christ."* (Philippians 1:6)
>
> *"For as a man (or woman) thinketh in his heart, so is he."* (Proverbs 23:7)
>
> *"For I know the thoughts that I think toward you, says the Lord, thoughts of peace and not of evil, to give you a future and a hope. Then you will call upon Me and go and pray to Me, and I will listen to you. And you will seek Me and find Me, when you search for Me with all your heart."* (Jeremiah 29:11-13)

Women often enter into marriage relationships not knowing who they are or the person they have married. When a woman does not know who she is and does not value her self-worth, it is not difficult for her to accept herself as who someone else says she is.

Perhaps man does not accept you, but you are accepted in the Beloved by God. He wonderfully and gloriously made you as His workmanship. God wants you to cry out against emotional, verbal, or physical abuse.

Satan wants to wear you down with foolishness to oppress you, to distract you from God's purpose and God's love. God's Word in Ephesians 5:6-7 instructs, "Let no one deceive you with empty words, for because of these things the wrath of God comes upon the sons of disobedience. Therefore, do not be partakers with them."

II Timothy 2:23 tells us to avoid foolish and ignorant disputes, knowing that they generate strife.

Why do some husbands try to dwindle their wives down to the lowest common denominator? Often it is to gain their sense of control and hide their own insecurities. If she believes that she is nothing good, her dependence and acceptance of his control can become absolute. A man of this character will try to evacuate all loved ones from her life by finding fault and developing problems with family members and friends. Very little association with others is allowed, and he is very creative in manipulating circumstances to minimize outside interaction. Thus, he develops a closed family system – their own little world, with him as ruler and king. No life, vision, or ideas will penetrate this family system and his hierarchy will begin construction.

Commonly, a person with this personality pattern is said to be narcissistic or to have Narcissistic Personality

Disorder, or even more serious, a Destructive Narcissistic Personality Disorder. These people, usually men, are consumed with unreal perceptions of unlimited success, power, or beauty, and desire continuous admiration and attention from selective sources. Narcissistic people take pride in being snobs. Because of their strong need for admiration, they will often be involved in extramarital relationships to maintain their grandiosity.

Usually, early childhood relationships influence this type of personality. Perfectionist parents could have been so concerned about these children's imperfections that their sense of real self was attacked, ignored, or assaulted. These children sometimes develop as people who are so driven to achieve that they never develop to the point of regarding the needs of others. Criticism or disapproval leads them into dominating anger and/or defensive fury because it suggests they're condescending from their flawlessness. Appearance is more important to them than feelings or substance because power and wealth cover up their low self-image.

In order to survive when interacting with narcissistic people, you must set firm boundaries. Do not sway from your decisions in response to their demands. Set a firm limit on how long and how often you will listen to their self-centered, controlling conversation. If they respond to your decisions with anger or blame, do not allow emotional blackmail and guilt. Your time and feelings are insignificant to them. Therefore, you must maintain their significance to you. Make your responses quietly, but firmly and with control.

Continuous interaction with this personality can make you feel depressed, irritable, devalued, and worthless. Sometimes, with this personality, the only way to cope is to end the relationship.

If you identify yourself as having this personality type or disorder, God can give you the heart and the knowledge to change. Maybe you are a victim to this narcissistic personality disorder. Ask God to guide you to additional resources that can teach you how to have control over these satanic forces in your life. Allow God to restore your "Freedom to Be – You."

## *Freedom to Be – "You"*

Three weeks of vacation
And when I returned
Sadness and depression
Within me burned
Why at this point in time
Would my emotions take this turn?
My family, my sister's family
Traveled to California in a nice, big van
To return drained and stressed out
Just could not understand
Later when my healing process began
I began to realize
That I had been passive and dishonest
Across many of those miles
Instead, I should have communicated truth in love
Not passive, not aggressive
But assertive style
Examples:
When asked, "Are you ready to stop
Traveling for the night?"
Although I may have wanted to stop in a different city
I would be phony and say, "Sure, that's all right."

"Beverly, would you like
to eat Chinese food this time?"
I replied, "That sounds good"
When right then eating Chinese food
Was the last preference in my mind

Want to shop for souvenirs today?
I said, "Cool"
When I really wanted to spend the day
in the whirlpool

Assertiveness is an honest way
Of expressing your thoughts,
opinions, and wishes
In spite of what controlling,
aggressive people might tell you
It's really all right to act in your own best interest
And when others do the same, don't resist – listen

You will feel better about yourself
When you are being truthful, not lying
Not being emotionally dishonest
And self-denying
Using self control in your daily situation
Being real in your responses and communication
As a passive person your first thought
Is, "What do people want me to say?"

But emotionally you will feel bound,
lack self-respect and creativity
When you handle life that way

God said let your yeah be yeah
And your nay be nay
In other words, say what you mean
And mean what you say

Clearly stating how you really feel
Is appropriate, not a selfish act
Keeping your opinion to yourself
to avoid confronting others
Is only an omission of facts

Withdrawal, fear, dishonest
Without open heart communication
Will further set the real issue back

Corrupt communication is impure and denies
Honest communication is true, edifies
Corrupt communication centers on man
Truthful communication induces
God's purpose and plan

So do not be passive
To get social support
Consider your needs, judgments,
and opinions meaningful priority
Or God's purpose and plan for you will abort

When you are able to express your views
And listen to others' views
That is assertive, not aggressive
So don't let anyone convince you
That you are being selfish

In Christ there is no condemnation
Against satan you must fight a good fight
You are God's workmanship,
wondrously and glorious made
Jesus' blood gave you your legitimate rights
You have been bought with a price
Inability to use truthful expression
Surfaces oppression
Which can form a runway for depression

Unto others do as you would have them to do
But do not allow them to take and don't you give up
Your freedom to be "YOU."

## THE BROWN PLANT BODY ROBED IN WHITE

> *"Do you not know that you are the temple of God and that the Spirit of God dwells in you? If anyone defiles the temple of God, God will destroy him. For the temple of God is holy, which temple you are."* (1 Corinthians 3:16-17)
>
> *"Do not be deceived, God is not mocked; for whatever a man sows, that he will also reap. For he who sows to his flesh will of the flesh reap corruption, but he who sows to the Spirit will of the Spirit reap everlasting life."* (Galatians 6:7-8)

In my own experience, I did not realize what a bondage cigarette smoking was until I got ready to quit. Because I was not a heavy smoker, I thought that I could quit whenever I wanted to. For Christians, smoking will not send you to hell, but it will certainly dim your light. This is because it associates you with something that is common to non-Christians or "the world." However, with all of the negative statistics that have been discovered through research, nicotine is an unhealthy substance for your body and can lead you to early death.

Not only did the reality of cigarette smoking as a bondage become obvious to me in my own experience, but also in my friends and family members. Two co-workers, in particular, were diagnosed with lung cancer and were told that they only had a short time to live. During that time, they were very afraid and wanted to live. My family and church family dedicated themselves to consistent prayer for each of them, and God raised them up. A few months later, one of these ladies came to have lunch with me, and when she reached for an ashtray, my heart fell to my feet in devastation. Truly, I could not believe that after her near death experience, she began smoking again with full knowledge that cigarette smoking stimulates cancer cells. Within one year, she died from cancer. I was advised that the other co-worker's cancer was in remission. Unfortunately, she went back to her old habits also and was dead within the year. Several of my family members had similar experiences. What bondage!

Did you know that cigarette smoking is linked not only to lung cancer, larynx cancer, and chronic bronchitis, but to leukemia, cataracts, pneumonia, and cancers of the kidney, pancreas, stomach, and cervix? The yearly average of American smoking-related deaths is 440,000. Since 1964, the Surgeon General reports twelve million Americans have died from smoking. Reports conclude that low-nicotine, low tar cigarettes are no less deadly. Consider these statistics and preserve your body so that you will give yourself more time for God's purpose. Do not be a victim of the "Brown Plant Body Robed In White."

## *Brown Plant Body Robed in White*

Brown plant body robed in white
Waiting to be lit so that
it can be sucked and absorbed as tar
and nicotine
Into the lungs of its victims
Lights on dormant cancer cells
Awakens them out of their slumber
Builds barriers between users and non-users
Causes inhabitants of
smoke free buildings to stand out in
below zero temperatures to
draw in death
Dims the light of Christians
Drawn to the brown plant body robed in white
Not recognized as bondage
until the victim tries to quit
Over, over, over, over
Quit, start back, quit, start back,
quit, and start back
Smelly clothes, smelly mouth,
yellow teeth, brown teeth,wrinkled skin
Facial features aged far beyond years
Some body parts decay

Others have to be removed
Nothing stops the victim's relationship
with the brown plant
body robed in white
An inseparable bond
Stroke, heart attack, throat cancer,
lung cancer – interrupts
the relationship only temporarily
As soon as stabilization begins,
the relationship must resume
Too often the only permanent
intruder is death
In the relationship between
the brown plant body  robed in
white and its victims
But he or she who Jesus,
the Son of God, sets free
Is free indeed
There is nothing too hard for God
This I know
For I was set free –
from the brown plant body robed in white
From victim – to victor –
Praise Jesus

# ENEMY ON THE LOOSE

*"Wine is a mocker, strong drink is a brawler, and whoever is led astray by it is not wise."* (Proverbs 20:1)

*"Who has woe? Who has sorrow? Who has contentions? Who has complaints? Who has wounds without cause? Who has redness of eyes? Those who linger long at the wine, Those who go in search of mixed wine. Do not look on the wine when it is red, when it sparkles in the cup, when it swirls around smoothly. At last it bites like a serpent and stings like a viper. Your eyes will see strange things. And your heart will utter perverse things. Yes, you will be like one who lies down in the midst of the sea, Or like one who lies at the top of the mast, saying: 'They have struck me, but I was not hurt. They have beaten me, but I did not feel it. When shall I awake, that I may seek another drink?' "* (Proverbs 23:29-35)

Alcohol is a drug – and a powerfully addictive one. My inspiration for this message was a result of watching several family members destroy their lives and their bodies through the addiction of alcohol.

One relative had her tongue removed because of cancer. After that, she would consume the alcohol through a dropper at the back of her throat.

Another loved one dove full-force into alcoholism to numb the depression of grief. Of course, he became more depressed because alcohol is a depressant.

In 2000, there were approximately 85,000 deaths caused by either excessive or unsafe drinking in the U.S., making alcohol the third leading actual cause of death (Mokdad, 2004). Vehicle accidents, drownings, homicides, suicides, falls, burns, rapes, and sexual assaults are often associated with alcohol abuse.

Alcohol – a drug – an "Enemy On the Loose."

## *An Enemy on the Loose*

An enemy on the loose – alcohol
One who lifts you up temporarily,
but only for a hard fall
Looses your speech
to say things you will regret
Looses your actions
and allows you to do things that will
make you ashamed of tomorrow
Looses your relationships
and runs loved ones out of your life
Looses you to fear
and carry a loaded gun at the risk of
killing those around you
Even those special babies
that you love so much
Looses you to drive under its influences
at the risk of killing
yourself and others in your path
Makes your life full of such dark secrets
that you no longer welcome the presence
of close relatives that love you
Looses a spirit of unhappiness
when you should be rejoicing in God's miracles

Looses a spirit of unfaithfulness
to the wife of your youth
Looses you from acting
as a child of God and causes you to
act as one of satan's children

Looses shame – alcohol
Looses division – alcohol
Looses your mind – alcohol
Looses your liver  - alcohol
Looses your stomach – alcohol
Looses your home – alcohol
Looses your children – alcohol

Your children's children
Children's children – Generations
And generations following
An enemy on the loose – alcohol
Alcohol, I command you,
by the power of the shed blood of Jesus
Loose my people and let them go!

# 6

# $\mathscr{G}$RACE FOR GODLY COVERINGS

**"O**H, MY GODLY Coverings! As Anointed and Wise As They Be – Flood My Soul With Such Freedom – To Pursue My Destiny!"

*-Beverly Armstrong, Author*

God has always provided covering for mankind, beginning with the cloud covering of the Israelites while parting Egypt en route to a land of milk and honey. Further and continuous coverings are in place by the Trinity through the Word of God, the Holy Spirit, and the Blood of Jesus. God provides us covering through people, such as parents, spouses, pastors, and other spiritual leadership. Godly coverings are essential for our development.

As I embark upon defining the characteristics of my spiritual coverings, each are individual, but yet have some brilliant commonalities. One commonality is a steadfast walk with God, in spite of all discouraging obstacles, devastating situations, and dramatic losses. Their beneficial contributions to my life and my ministry, to name a few, are: not crowding my time and space; never-ending support of my writing ministry; absolute freedom to grow and bloom, providing a peaceful environment so that God's messages can flow through me; spiritual guidance, prayer covering, rightly dividing the Word of Truth; and establishing structure in the church so that it can be a haven of God's manifested presence, not an operation of the enemy. All of these attributes and more have helped nurture me for my God-ordained assignment.

## HUSBAND: A GODLY COVERING
## AS CHRIST LOVES THE CHURCH

> *"Husbands, love your wives, just as Christ also loved the church and gave Himself for her, that He might sanctify and cleanse her with the washing of water by the Word."* (Ephesians 5:25-26)

Prior to my deliverance, I was a self-induced Christian doormat. This was because I had, unknowingly, established my own righteousness in some cases and had not submitted to the righteousness of God. This emotionally unhealthy lifestyle came to a head and, consequently, I entered into a season of depression. During my first counseling session, I was told that everything that had happened to me, I had allowed to happen. In many situations, I did not understand how I could be in God's will without surrendering to all of the demands of others.

Fascinatingly, through it all, my husband never supported this doormat mentality. He always encouraged me not to allow him or anyone else to manipulate me, control my mind, or make me feel bad about my decisions or about speaking the truth in love. On the contrary, he continued to assure me that the first person I was to please was myself. Today we live in an era of inappropriate male domination, primitive interpretation of the meaning of "headship and submission," and increased incidents of domestic violence. Yet, my husband's position has always been that I have the mind of Christ and that, if I am obedient to God's voice, God will be pleased, I will be plased, and he will be pleased. He also supports that if I am not pleased, more than likely, God is not pleased either.

My husband's support of my freedom and individuality is characteristic of something that I recently heard on the radio regarding headship. This radio minister said that headship should be like that of a fountainhead. It waters the fountain continuously until the fountain reaches its full potential. Truthfully, that is the way my husband's headship has been in his 22 years of grooming me to be a vessel equipped for ministry in God's Kingdom.

His covering has always been one of protection, provision, and always accommodating, not dominating. Therefore, submitting to him has been a natural response, not one of toil, pain, and oppression. Because I know that he is always looking out for my best interest, I trust him. Is he perfect? Of course not, but his heart towards me is pure and always considerate of my well-being. Even more significant, God is always in the center of us – Godly covering.

Just as Boaz covered Ruth prior to their relationship, my husband covered me also. The first time that he came to my house, my car would not start when we got ready to leave a choir singing engagement. He fixed it while I rode home with a friend, came by to bring me the keys, and went on his way. When the weather was snowy, I would know by the scraping that I would hear outside of my house. On his way to work, he would stop by my house, clean off my car, my driveway, and my walkway. When he finished, he would not even ring my doorbell. He would proceed on to his destination without expecting coffee, tea, or me. He never made demands on my time or my hospitality. After we came to the conclusion that it was God's plan for us to join our lives together, he made what to me was a peculiar request. He wanted to see all of my bills. In my single independence, I had no idea what he was up to. When I asked, he explained to me that he wanted to check out the interest rate on my bills. When he saw the interest rate, he was not pleased with it and immediately prepared a schedule for pay-off. *What a man!*

- Me – Always Covering
- My Livelihood – Always Covering

- My Peace of Mind – Always Covering
- My Mother – Always Covering
- The Children – Always Covering
- The Grandchildren – Always Covering
- The Family – Always Covering

There is nothing that I ever wanted, nothing I wanted to do, no place I have wanted to go that has not been supported by my husband when it was within his means to make it happen. For twenty-two years, I have never asked him to do anything for me that he would not do unless God led him otherwise. What a man!

All praises be to the King of Kings! In the planning of our wedding, purchase of our home and vacation property, and trip decisions, we have always been on one accord. What a mighty God! What a man – a Godly covering.

## *Always – All Ways*

Charles,
When I think of you as a husband,
I just don't know where to start
In 22 years not a day has gone by
That you did not do something
To warm my heart

When I think of you as a person
There is so much I could say
But the one single word that stands when I think of you
Is the word ALWAYS

Always encouraging
No matter what the situation
Able to see light at the end of the tunnel
Through planning and determination

Always doing what's best for the family
Through a heart of love
With a quiet and humble spirit
That could come only from God above

Always holding on to your steadfast faith

Through sickness, trials, and pain

Never, ever doubting that God

Will bring us through again


I could go on and on and on

But there's much too much for one page

Your expressions of love are too numerous to name

But the sum of your deeds of kindness and lifestyle of faith

Husband, father, grandfather, brother, son-in-law, man of

God, teacher, friend

Is the dynamic of


ALL WAYS.

## MOTHER: A GODLY COVERING

> *"Train up a child in the way he should go,
> And when he is old he will not depart from
> it."* (Proverbs 22:6)

There are many ways that my mother could have turned when she became a widow at age twenty-one with a three-year-old (me), a five-year-old, and a seven-year-old. My father had died suddenly at the age of twenty-one with military tuberculosis while in the United States Army. Thanks be unto God, she decided to let us live with my grandmother, a Godly woman, who had moved from Chicago to the little bitty city, Three Rivers, Michigan.

Yes, Mama could have made many choices, being just barely an adult. However, she chose to live in an environment that would be best for her babies. At first, she returned to Chicago often. Then she settled down and adjusted her life as a country, small-town, full-time Mom.

While we lived in my grandmother's house, going to church was a natural, consistent part of our lives. Sunday's schedule was walking to Sunday school and church in the morning, walking home afterwards, and walking back to church for evening service. We were taught to love God, to have faith in God, and to believe His Word.

After a few years, my mother moved us into a flat of our own. Not long after that, she purchased a brand new ranch-style home for us. It took great vision for her to undertake the responsibility of being a homeowner.

When my grandfather had a stroke, my mother took care of him until it got to be too much of a hardship for us. After that, she put him in a nearby nursing facility and visited him often until his death. Later, when my grandmother became ill and unable to live alone, my mother added another room on to our home so that she could be taken care of in our house.

My mother made our lives good lives, even to this day. Because our home was without a male image, she encouraged my brother to enlist in the Air Force. When my sister wanted to get married, Mom went all out in planning her beautiful wedding. When I decided that I wanted to go to business school in Chicago, she supported me in that endeavor. When she found out that I had gotten married without even telling her, she did not condemn me, but rose to the occasion in love. There was absolutely nothing that went on in the lives of her children that she was not there to support, even if support meant chastisement, sharing wisdom, or letting us know that we were wrong. She has just always been there for her children, her grandchildren, great-grandchildren, and now, great-great grandchildren.

Above all else, she is, I believe, a woman after God's own heart. Yes, she has fallen, as we all have. Yet she never allowed seasons to go by without reconnecting her life with her God. Because God never gave up on her, she never gives up on people. Her conversations to others are never condemning, but full of the brightness and insight of hope. She is a woman of great character and above-average integrity, living and instilling in her children the slogan that anything worth doing is worth doing well. This widowed young lady did not allow us to enter questionable environments. Instead, she raised us in the fear and admonition of God. She did not expose her children to the risk of abuse. No man lived with us unless he was her husband. She did not work until I was in high school, and when we came home from school, dinner was cooked and waiting for us. My mother, a Godly covering, still influences the generations as they come.

As parents, we are the covering for our children. Our covering can protect them from exposure of ungodly attacks. What we expose them to and allow them to be exposed to can chart the course of their lives and generations following.

Undoubtedly, my mother takes her role of mother very seriously, encouraging her children in the midst of the good, the bad, and the ugly. Mom encouraged me to reach out to and befriend a wonderful guy who has now been my loving husband for twenty-two years. Now she is "stately eighty."

As her child, I rise up and call her "blessed" because she blesses the world with her wisdom and unselfish, unconditional love. Praise be unto God for blessing me with such an awesome mother from my birth until now.

> *"Honor thy father and mother that thy days will be long upon the land ..."* (Exodus 20:12)

## *We Rise Up and Call You "Blessed"*

On Thanksgiving Day, 1925
In Cincinnati, Ohio
Laura and Ambrose Humes
Had a little girl
Her name was Estella because
she is a star
Her presence rocked the world

At an early age, she moved to Chicago
When her parents relocated there
Later she fell in love with Mansfield Patterson
They got married
As a result, Mansfield Jr., Lorraine,
and Beverly are here

Mansfield Sr. went to the army
Then went to the hospital –
Mom thought he was just sick a little
But at that time there was
no cure for Tuberculosis
And at 21 she became a widow

So life for her has not been easy
But God always brought her through
After much tragedy, even the death of a son
She survived, reached out to others, and grew
Mom always has a deep concern about people
Her love reaches so far that she never gives up
When her loved ones reach their lowest points in life
Mom will stand in the gap and tell satan – ENOUGH!

Her love energizes her to reach down and pick others up
There is nothing you can do to make her love go away
She always recognizes the good in people and
When she sees the bad, believes God for their deliverance,
Keeps the faith and prays

She is always considerate of others
Considers others before herself
You can hear the pleasure in her voice
When she is able
To reach out to family, friends, and community and help

Yes, we could go on and on about this "stately lady"
Oh, yes, she has her ways
But she daily lives a life in which her children can rise up

and call her blessed
To Estella Patmon and to her God
I give her Honor and Praise

# UNTO MT. ZION

The first sermon that I heard Bishop Charles L. Middleton preach was "The Making Of A Nation" at the Greater Morning Star Missionary Baptist Church in Mt. Clemens, Michigan in 1982. At that time, I was under the awesome pastorate of Bishop J. Douglas Wiley. That message, indeed, took my spiritual growth to a new level in God. Although I discerned that Bishop Middleton truly had a pastor's heart, I never dreamed that one day he would be my pastor. Later, after Bishop Wiley relocated, God gave my husband and I special favor and assigned Bishop Middleton as our spiritual covering. And cover he does, in all areas of our lives, preaching, teaching, supporting our personal endeavors, praying for our sick, encouraging us and other families, even those who have moved on to other ministries.

Undoubtedly, the heights that Bishop Middleton has been able to reach in God are because of the woman of extraordinary faith and perseverance who is at his side, Co-Pastor Mary E. Middleton. Together, they stand as they walk out their covenant relationship and minister to the world. Co-Pastor Mary always has a Word from God in her belly. In this era, many pastors and their wives are unapproachable and far removed from the people they serve. These pastors, however, are approachable and personably connected to their congregation. Much of their focus is on the subject that faith and covenant relationships are two areas high on God's list of priorities; without faith, it is impossible to please God. Throughout the Bible, God stresses the importance of covenant relationships.

To be in covenant relationships is to be in fellowship, harmony, and dedication to one another, with undivided loyalty to one another. In that same vein, covenant bonds are another source of support that will keep us in line with God's will and His purpose for our lives. As situations occur and things happen that, in the natural, make us want to relocate to another ministry, the commitment of a covenant relationship will allow us to "hang on in there" until and unless God directs us to make a change. To maintain good covenant relationships, we must learn to communicate even when we do not agree and make sure that we are always open for communication from others. Also, we must resist any communication or action that will cause division. To ensure that a covenant relationship is maintained, prayer is essential. Also, in order to keep the covenant fresh and alive in our hearts, we must center our focus on the vision, teaching, and direction of the covenant heads. Even if we do not agree with the actions of our leaders, we must respect and honor their God-given positions. Covenant keeping not only demands responsibility, but also accountability. Accountability centers on maintaining lifestyles that are directed by the Holy Spirit and are in harmony with God's Word.

Our pastors lead us in serving in spite of opposition and physical conditions. Many of Co-Pastor Mary's slogans have led me through difficult times and situations. Two of my favorites are: "It's a walk" and "You see and you don't see." When it comes to food, "it's <u>got</u> to be <u>fresh</u>." Slogans from the Bishop that continuously bless my life are, "We're all in the big room" (of improvement), "Act like God told you the truth," and his constant reminder to us; "We are God's visible representatives in the earth."

In my personal walk with God, I realize why God and my pastors emphasize covenant. There have been times when my flesh felt ready for a break from the local assembly. Yet, I would go to fulfill the covenant duties that God had assigned to me. Each time, I was so very blessed, rejuvenated, and thankful that I was in the right place at the right time doing the right thing with the right people.

Here is a salute to Bishop Charles L. Middleton and Co-Pastor Mary E. Middleton as they lead God's people by the Spirit of God with the shield of faith and the covenant of love.

## *Unto Mt. Zion*

When we came Unto Mt. Zion New Covenant
Seeking the will of the Lord
We had tracked Bishop Middleton down
And just dropped by
We knew that through him,
God's voice would be heard

Oh, but when we stepped through the door
God's presence radiated to the max
Now, I'm not trying to impress anyone
I am merely stating the facts

Everyone was praising and worshipping God
The Spirit was moving from front to back
Then a lady danced all the way to the offering table
Who else but Minister Carolyn Sapp

We knew before we came that Bishop had a message
Among our favorites was "The Making of a Nation"
But in addition to the powerful Word in this place
The whole service was a Holy Ghost Manifestation

After our first visit
We continued to seek God's face
But we knew deep down in our Spirit
That we would return to this place
For Mt. Zion is truly the Place of the Presence
As Elder Crouch says so affectionately
For His Presence permeates every fiber of our service
His Spirit takes control – there is liberty

Even as awesome as Bishop Middleton's ministry is
When Co-Pastor Mary's feet hit the floor
Anything that is not of God gets to fleeing
Satan's very imps know what is in store

She always comes forth with fresh oil
Teaching and preaching unity
To support the vision of the Man of God
And his focus on Covenant Community

They are both concerned about how we treat one another
And others who walk through the door
They want us to identify through how we act
That we are very different from the world

So with double honor we must bless these pastors
And I'm not trying to be funny
But honor means more than syrupy words
It means time and it means money

To you, the great people of Mt. Zion
Who are never satisfied with the status quo
Whatever level God blesses us to reach
You always have a higher goal

For we know that in Christ
We must always progress
Always time to get busy
No time for mess

First on the agenda is the business of the Father
Bishop says if we don't take the message to the street
That we may as well close the doors
Why bother?

For a dying world is waiting for what we have inside
The harvest is ripe, but the laborers are few
Our candles are not to hide

Under God, Bishop has chosen Full Gospel
As our Spiritual covering
For it is a powerful move of God –
Get with it! Quit pondering!
Follow the move, follow the gift
When He moves, you move
Don't miss the shift

Now if you're all dressed up
in a wedding gown
We may look up
And you may not be around

But if you don't mind putting on war clothes
Giving satan fits as his territory we foreclose
If you'll get in the trenches of Spiritual warfare
Willing to fight radically against the powers of the air
Then YOU hang on in here
YOU just keep on trying
Because that what it's all about
UNTO MT. ZION

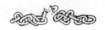

# FULL GOSPEL BAPTIST CHURCH FELLOWSHIP

God in heaven knows that I am ecstatic about not only the free spirit of the Full Gospel Baptist Church Fellowship International, but also about the order that the fellowship has added to the churches under its covering. It is not just a denomination – it is a powerful move of the Almighty God. When my Pastor Bishop J. Douglas Wiley left our church to pursue other ministry options, I did not even know the name of his new affiliation. But one day after he had relocated to Louisiana, I was in route to church and I heard on the radio the words "Full Gospel Baptist Church" for the first time! Joy and excitement overwhelmingly leaped within me.

For too long, I had witnessed the model of church government that allowed a few planned and manipulated acts to actually control the structure and standards of the local church. Another order that had the church weighted was tradition. Just as I, and many others, were tired of tradition, others fought untiringly for its continuance under the concept that, "We've always done it this way." As my Pastor, Bishop Charles L. Middleton Sr. often says, "If you don't understand me, don't misunderstand me." Certainly, traditions are in order when they line up with God's Word. When the tradition limits God's Word, the move of God's Spirit and the spiritual functioning of God's people, however, it is outside of Kingdom order. Tradition of man is another weapon of the enemy to distract us from and terminate God's purpose in our lives.

Thanks be unto God that the Full Gospel Baptist Church Fellowship International under the leadership of our Presiding Bishop Paul S. Morton and Elder Debra Morton has surpassed all ungodly tradition and released a powerful move of God. The Full Gospel Spirit has set the captive free and given sight to those blinded and bound by tradition as they continually reach for even more of the fullness of God. Praise God for the spiritual support system with accountability to its Pastors, leaders and churches. No limits.

Thank you, Bishop Paul Morton, Elder Debra Morton, Bishops' Council, Tiers of Leadership, and the Full Gospel Baptist Church Fellowship International in its entirety for giving us all a right to choose so that we can "Change A Generation." Truly, I consider it the favor of God that has allowed us to be a part of and under the covering of this awesome Fellowship, this Powerful Move of God.

*A Tribute to the Full Gospel Baptist*
*Church Fellowship*
*(A Powerful Move of God)*

It's glorious, electrifying, sets you aglow
You know that it is different
I mean from the first, you just know

It quickens your spirit
Sets your soul aflight
It just gives you assurance
that everything is all right

My first experience
was at Fountain of Truth
I was flying so high
I was on a spiritual roof

Or like soaring with the eagles
Above all my worldly cares
Into God's presence
The Heavenly sphere

It draws, it pulls, it tugs at your inner man
Makes you return for more whenever you can
You realize that this free spirit is no fiction
And these people, like you, are just tired of tradition

Ready for the move of the Spirit of God
To glow, grow, and go while in Jesus to trod
No muss, no fuss, don't care where or when
Just to lift up Jesus as He draws men

No bondage, no reservation, no tradition, no hoax
Spirit just moving from coast to coast
Just moving, just moving, never quenched
Filling of the Holy Ghost,
People just getting drenched

Went to Mt. Zion New Covenant
Same way over there
I tell you in this movement
God breaks out everywhere

These folks are serious
They're not joshing or playing
They are seeking God's will

Living holy and praying
I went to the State fellowship
A concert, you hear one, you hear them all
But even the concert was different
And it was not because of the crowd
That was from wall to wall
This concert was different, I tell you
You had to have been there to understand
That it represented the fullness of God
Not something done by man
And that choir had a real attitude
They had not come to play
They came to represent a blood-bought life
That Jesus had washed their sins away

They praised God's name with a vengeance
War on satan and his demons
The glory of the Lord was upon them
Their faces were glowing and beaming

At the meeting of the State the people were kind
Again, the Spirit just blew my mind
I knew by then that I was hooked
I could not turn back by hook or by crook

A group that although under much criticism
They stare satan in the eye and say, "Oh, well
You can try to water God's gospel down
But it's still holiness or hell!"

And then a few weeks later
The Women of Excellence met
I did not know how much more
Fired up this thing could get
As soon as I walked in the church that night
God's presence was radiating, His glory
Shining bright

Oh, yes, it was Women of Excellence,
Holy Ghost flowing
Like a river
And leave it to this move of God,
men too were in the house
Being delivered

And just when I thought
There couldn't be much more
Holy laughter broke out
Deliverance was like a roar
You could see it, you could hear it

you could feel it from within
And then it would break out all over again
Prophesy, healing, salvation taking place
Lumps being healed right in front of my face

These had to be some crazy folks
I no longer had to roam
Because I grew up in God
under Bishop Wiley
And I was right at home

I knew when I first walked in
Mt. Zion New Covenant
God had it going on, I could see
And I knew in my heart that I would be back
Whenever I had a chance to be

I mean spiritual gifts were flowing
Prophesy, translation
Tongues, Word of Knowledge
All kinds of affirmation
All I could do was sit and gaze
Feast on this free Spirit
In joyous amaze

Pastor Middleton

preaching God's Word with power

Getting us ready for that great day

Preaching like we don't know day nor hour

Not acting like it was far, far away

I thought as I marveled

This thing is for real

It is according to knowledge

It is not just a zeal


I joined there, I love it there

Not perfect, but see

It's what I need, it's what I want

It's the church that God gave me

Then I visited New Birth

I had heard a lot about it

They are excited about Jesus

And not afraid to shout it

Ready for whatever God wanted to do

Ready to act on God's word like it's true

I had never seen anything like it before

Walking miles from their cars

to get to the church door

So this move of God that I've been describing

In case you don't already know
Is the Full Gospel Baptist Church Fellowship
It has set the world aglow

When Bishop Wiley
and Life Center's Praise Team
Came to GMS
They came for a sad occasion
But the way they worshipped and gave praise to God
I knew that their mission was to change a generation
And when I want to New Orleans to Life Center
I certainly was not disappointed
The fellowship, the spirit, the worship, the Word
Everything was anointed
Excellence was in the air
To make sure God's program went right
The flavor of love, warmth, and vision manifested
Unity in the Spirit was in sight

And last but not least Conference 96
I was blessed – Jesus and me had a ball
And I will not be consumed by
"The Enemy Called Average"
As I respond to my "Last Call"

Thank you, Lord, for a fresh, clean start

This Full Gospel Baptist Church Fellowship

has won my heart

I'm not putting others down

I just want to be a part

I will never settle for a church of tradition

Where my spirit keeps wishing and wishing and wishing

To see God in His fullness, His Spirit set free

For where the Spirit of God flows, there is liberty


Thank you, Bishop Morton for being the one

That God used

For Baptists to be a part of the fullness of God

Giving us a right to choose

# $\mathscr{E}$PILOGUE

These Messages of Deliverance were written
according to the Word of God and revealed to me
by the Spirit of God through experiences as I walk with
God and experience intimate fellowship with Him
through Jesus Christ.
It is my fervent prayer and expectation that the impartation
of these messages into your life will tear down strongholds
and destroy any yokes and bondages.   My declaration is
that,
as new light and new freedom penetrate your mind, body,
and spirit,
the divine will of God for your life will illuminate
so that you will be released to fulfill your
God-ordained purpose…

BY GRACE

# About the Author

BEVERLY ARMSTRONG is a renaissance woman, an energetic personality, called for such a time as this. God has gifted her to function in her calling as servant of God, worshipper, teacher, Deaconess, wife, mother, grandmother and clinical therapist. For years, this author has had a burning passion for God's people to walk in total deliverance and evidenced this commitment as she self-published her first book, *Poetic Messages of Deliverance*. This author's writings are profound demonstrations and reflections of God's Word as they honor, enlighten and edify by producing purpose, promise and possibility.

This author's unique gift of expression was recognized by My Brother's Keeper Benevolent Society, Inc. (MBKBSI), affording them no choice but to invite Beverly to join their on-air staff weekly with *Moments of Inspiration*. During this 6-month period, comments poured in weekly from the Detroit Metropolitan area listening audience about the effect that deliverance had on their lives.

God inspired Beverly to add knowledge and credentials to her spiritual, vocational calling. She attained a Bachelor's degree in Psychology and a Master's in Social Work, both through Wayne State University, in Detroit, Michigan.

This author is a recipient of the Graduate professional Scholarship, Margret Hummberger Private Scholarship, the Senior Scholar's Award, and is a member of the Golden Key National Honor Society.

Through her own experience of deliverance, God has endowed Beverly with compassion and sensitivity to walk in deliverance and spread God's message of deliverance to others. She has studied the principles of her own deliverance in order to formulate them into learnable dialogue for her readers. Yet, she has a strong, uncompromising belief that only the Word of God through the Spirit of God can break up the fallow ground of the hearts of man.

Beverly's affiliations with the Called and Ready Writers and Poetic Justice for God have afforded her great ministry opportunities and cultivation.

# Bibliography and Resource Room

American Psychiatric Association (DSM-IV), *Diagnostic and Statistical Manual of Mental Disorders,* < http://www.psych. org/> (2004).

"Assertive Communication." www.twu.edu/counseling/ SelfHelp011.html

Assertiveness. <http://www.mindspring.com>

Bible.com, *What Does The Bible Say About Choosing A Mate?,* <www.bible.com/bibleanswers> (1995-2005). "The Value of Rest." www.bodybuilding.com/fun/behav2

Brian, Juan, "Dialogue: Is Premarital Sex Wrong?" <JuanBrian@aol.com>

Bridges, Jerry, *The Pursuit of Holiness.* Colorado Springs: Nav Press, 1978, 1996.

Burns, David D. *Feeling Good: New Mood Therapy. New York:* Avon Books, An Imprint of HarperCollins Publishers, 1980.

Byerly, Paul and Lori, "Oxytocin in Women: The Bridge Between Touch and Sex." <www.themarriagebed.com> (1997-2005).

Counseling Center – Assertive Communication. <www.twu-edu/0-5/counseling/SelfHelp011.html>

Counseling Center, *Assertiveness*, <www.couns.uiuc.ed/Brochures/assertive.htm>

Counseling Briefs, *Emotional Healing,* <http://alternative-counseling.org/c-briefs/eh-steps.html>

Christianity Yesterday and Today, *Let Us Make Man In Our Image,* 25 September 1999, <www.purechristianity.org/> (25 September 1999).

Daily, Jon, LCSW, CADC, "Distorted Thinking." <www.recoveryhappens.com/distorted%20 thinking.html>

"Emotional Abuse and Your Faith", "The Bible On Abuse and Violence", "Is Divorce the Answer to Spousal Abuse?" "Domestic Abuse in the Lord's House." eaandfaith.blogspot.com/2005/02 silent-killer-of-christian-marriages.html

Fundamental Evangelistic Association, *Baptismal Regeneration and Bible Salvation*, <www.fundamentalbiblechurch.org> (Founded 1928).

Furr, LeRoy Allen, *Exploring Human Behavior and the Social* Environment. Allyn & Bacon, 1997

"The Holy Bible"   King James Version

"The Holy Bible"  Woman Thou Art Loosed Version

Hoy, Lynette J. and Yeschek, Steve, "Counsel Care Connection." <www.counselcareconnection.org/services. asp>  (2001-2006).
Idolaters Anonymous. "Idolatry." <www.luc.edu/faculty/ pmoser/idolanon>

The Institute For Life Enrichment, *Christian Tree of Life.* < http://www.tifle.com> (2000-2006).

Pastor Vic, "Lying Against the Truth,"  <www. vicporterministries.com/leadership.html>

The Peacemaker: A Biblical Guide to Resolving Personal Conflict.
A Puritan's Mind. *Carnal Christian?* <http://www. apuritansmind.com>

*The Man Of Soul.*  <http://www.worldinvisible.com>

Huntington, S.S., W.H., "Image of God in Man," <www. grace-for-today.com/1229.htm>

Hubert,MJ, "Wings As Eagles Ministries," <www. wingsaseaglesministries.org/godsway.html> (4 September 1999).

Michael C. Bain, *Blood.* 30 January 2005. <It-is-finished. blogspot.com> (30 January 2005).

PENN-Friends, *Assertive Behavior – An Outline. 11 September 1997.* <www.upenn.edu/fsap/assert.htm> (11 September 1997).

"Project Respect – Yes Means Yes – The Facts Marriage Romance.com – Is Premarital Sex Worth It?" www.yesmeansyes.com/modphp?mod

Queendom.com, *Assertiveness Test.* <www.queendom.com/tests/personality/assertiveness> (1996-2006).

"A Quick Christian Theology of Sex." wwwstmattsmamly,orgau/

"Sanctuary For the Abused." Abusesanctuary.blogspot.com Epigee Women's Health, *Human Reproduction* <www.epigee.org/guide/reproduction.html>

Seek God Ministries. *He Who Is Of God.* <http://www.seekgod.org/message/hearinggod.html> (1997-2006).

Seeq, *Anxiety Fact Sheet.* <www.brighter-tomorrow.com/anxiety-facts-information>

The Sermon Notebook, *Blood Is A Precious Substance.* 2003. <www.sermonnotebook.org/old/%20testament/Lev2017-11.htm> (2003).

"Sex Tips For Geeks: Sex and Consequences." www.catb. org//-esc/writing/sextips/consequences.html

Smalley, Gary, *Making Love Last Forever.* LifeWay Press, 1996.

Taj Anapol, Dr. Deborah Ph.D., *Become Healthy Now.com, The Blood Pathfinders for Kids, The Circulatory System, The Life Pump, The Circulatory System, Biology II Anatomy & Physiology Human (Male and Female) Reproductive Systems, Society, the Church and Same Sex Marriages, Why Sex Is Sacred,* <www.becomehealthynow.com/category/ bodycardioblood>

This Is A War. *Abuse.* <http://www.thisiswar.com/ AbuseEmotional.htm>

Wikipedia, the Free Encyclopedia. *How Beaches Are Formed.* <http://www.en.wikipedia.org/wiki/Beach>

Wikipedia, the Free Encyclopedia. *Oxytocin.* <http://www. en.wikipedia.org/wiki/Oxytocin>

Codependency. <http://joy2meu.com/codependency/. html>

<http://www.fundamentalbiblechurch.org/Tracts/fbcbaptr. htm>

Delivered by *Grace*

<http://www.marriageromance.com/stories> –
MarriageRomance.com

# Index

## A

Homeowner - 224
Homosexuality - 117-118
Honest communication - 132, 202
Hope - 28, 96, 124, 178, 196, 226
Hormone - 12, 92, 180
Humanness - 63
Humility - 55, 58, 132
    159, 163-165, 167, 171,
    174, 183, 197, 217-
    221, 225-226, 230
Husband - 8, 60, 120, 146, 153,
    155-159, 163-165,
    167, 171-174, 183,
    197, 217-223, 225-226, 230

I

Idolatry - 147, 153, 190, 253
Ignorant disputes - 197
Individuality - 218, 136
Infant environmental
Influences - 13
Inner man - 193, 239
Insignificant - 199
Intimacy - 174, 179, 181, 183-186
Intimate time - 155, 172

J

Jerk - 185
Jesus - 6-8, 10, 17, 24, 31, 34, 36-37,
    39, 41-44, 49, 50, 65-66, 68,
    71, 74, 80, 92, 96-97, 100,
    102, 105, 123, 126,
    130, 141-142, 144,
    146, 159, 166, 169, 172,

177, 178,
181, 187, 195-196, 203,
208, 212,
215, 240-241, 244-245, 247

K

Kingdom of darkness - 2, 34, 35,
    39, 65, 72, 98, 118,
    145, 147, 158

L

Liberty - 62, 108, 166, 234, 246
Liquid tissue - 64
Livelihood - 150, 219

M

Manipulate - 2, 59, 193, 217, 237
Marriage - 44, 105, 117-119, 130,
    146-148, 158, 179, 186, 196
"Married saved" - 171
Marrow of faith - 68
Mask - 137
Mature - 7, 12, 104-105, 109, 112
Mature love - 103
Mediation process - 54
Moral values - 147
Mother - 2, 12, 60, 65, 117-118, 146,
    156, 169, 219, 223-226
Murmur 169
Muscles - 92-93

# W

To order additional copies of *Delivered by Grace*, or to find out about other books by Beverly Armstrong or Zoë Life Publishing please visit our website www.zoelifepub.com.

A bulk discount of 35% off of the retail price is available when 12 or more books are purchased at one time for your men's ministry group, women's ministry group, workshop, or conference.

Zoë Life Publishing
P.O. Box 871066
Canton, MI 48187
(877) 841-3400
outreach@zoelifepub.com